ROSEANNE
ROSEANNADANNA'S

"HEY, GET BACK TO WORK!" BOOK

by
Roseanne Roseannadanna

with Lots o' Help from

Alan Zweibel

and

Gilda Radner

LONG SHADOW BOOKS
PUBLISHED BY POCKET BOOKS NEW YORK

Another *Original* publication of LONG SHADOW BOOKS

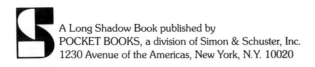

A Long Shadow Book published by
POCKET BOOKS, a division of Simon & Schuster, Inc.
1230 Avenue of the Americas, New York, N.Y. 10020

ISBN: 0-671-47394-8

First Long Shadow Books printing October, 1983

10 9 8 7 6 5 4 3 2 1

LONG SHADOW BOOKS and colophon are trademarks
of Simon & Schuster, Inc.

Printed in the U.S.A.

Cover photo: Edie Baskin
Design: Jacques Chazaud
Photo section and Scrapbook editor: Bob Pook
Photo researcher: Edd Hall
Hair: Lyn Quiyou
Make-up: Barbara Armstrong

Photo section: FPG/Ben McCall; FPG/Photoworld; Frederic Lewis, Inc.; FPG/
Photoworld; FPG/David Plowden; courtesy of Gilda Radner; Edie Baskin;
Frederic Lewis, Inc./Harold Lambert; FPG/Ralph Joosten; Edie Baskin; NBC
Photo; Wide World; Edie Baskin; UPI; Frederic Lewis, Inc./R. Gates; UPI; Edie
Baskin; Frederic Lewis, Inc.; UPI; Edie Baskin; UPI; Edie Baskin.

Toast o' the Town Scrapbook: Edie Baskin; UPI; Edie Baskin; UPI, Edie Baskin,
UPI; Wide World, Edie Baskin; Edie Baskin; UPI; Garry Trudeau; Edie Baskin,
UPI; Edie Baskin, UPI; Edie Baskin, UPI; Pat Oliphant; Edie Baskin, NBC Photo;
Al Hirschfeld/Margot Feiden Galleries, New York.

Acknowledgments

Thanks, but not a penny to:

BELLA ABZUG • GEORGE ACEVEDO • ROBERT ACKERMAN • AL'S LIMOUSINE • ALAN'S MOM & DAD • ALAN ALDA • ARLENE ALDA • ALISA ADLER • STEVEN ALDER • THE ALDETTES • ALFRAN-SOMERS • MEL ALLEN • FRANK ALOISE • CHARLES AMEND • LISBETH ANDERSON • ANDREA • ERIC ANGELSON • DALE ANGLUND • ROSIE APPLE • BARBARA ARMSTRONG • DESI ARNAZ • BEA ARTHUR • MARTY ASHER • PETER ASHKENAZE • SUSAN AST • RICHARD AVEDON • DAN AYKROYD • PETER AYKROYD • GRACE AYRSMAN • JANINE BABCOCK • ED BAILEY • DOREEN BAKER • DEAN BALIN • FRANK BALZAND • ANNE BANCROFT • ED BAND • SUSAN BARAN • FRANK BARRA • PETER BASIL • EDIE BASKIN • JULES BASS • STEPHANIE BATCHLEOR • BILLY BAXTER • ANNE BEATTS • AUNT BELLE • RONNIE BELLIZZI • RABBI BELSKY • JOHN BELUSHI • RICHARD BELZER • RICHARD BENJAMIN • LORRAINE BENNETT • EILEEN BERG • CANDICE BERGEN • MILTON BERLE • AUNT BERNICE • ANNETTE BIANCO • EARL BIGGETT • PAT BIRCH • DR. BLACK • KAREN BLACK • ALICE BLACKWELDER • CAROLE BLANKMAN • JEFF BLANKMAN • PEARL BLANKMAN • ROBIN BLANKMAN • SAMUEL BLANKMAN • GREG BLOCH • TONY BLOCK • ROY BLOUNT, JR. • THE BLUES BROTHERS • DIANE BLUMBERG • BOATY BOATWRIGHT • BOB & RAY • BOBY • PETER BOCHAN • TOBY BOCHAN • JULIAN BOND • WAYNE BOOHER • CAREN BORENSTEIN • KAREEN BOURSIER • HENRY BOYARSKY • PETER BOYLE • SENATOR BILL BRADLEY • DELMA BRADLEY • SHIRLEY BRAM • LUCA BRASI • BILL BRATTON • DORA BRAUN • JOSEPH BRAUN • DAVID BRENNER • JAY BRICK • THE BRILL BUILDING • BERNIE BRILLSTEIN • DAVID BRILLSTEIN • DEBBIE BRILLSTEIN • KATE BRILLSTEIN • LEE BRILLSTEIN • MICHAEL BRILLSTEIN • MOE BRILLSTEIN • NICHOLAS BRILLSTEIN • JOEL BRISKIN • BROADWAY VIDEO • TRICIA BROCK • LINDA BROCKINGTON • DR. BRONSTEIN • ALBERT BROOKS • MEL BROOKS • BROOKS VAN HORN • RICHIE BROWN • SUSAN BROWN • PAUL BRUBAKER • NICHOLAS BRUNO • MARK BUCHARD • COUSIN BUDDY • MICHAEL BUDMAN • MILTON BURAS • BARBARA BURNS • JACK BURNS • GARY BUSEY • BOGEY BUYSE • EMILE BUYSE • EVELYN BUYSE • JOHN CALIONE • JOHN CAGLIONE, JR. • STEVEN CALLAHAN • AL CAMOIN • CAMP MAPLEHURST • CAMP TAMAKWA • SUE ANN CAMPBELL • DYAN CANNON • DICK CAPRI • ROSEMARY CARDILLO • CANDY CARELL • LEN CARIOU • GEORGE CARLIN • JACKIE CARLIN • SANDRA CARNEGIE • DENNIS CARNEY • CAROL LEE CAROL • MARTHA CARSON • WAYNE CARSON • JOHN CARUSO • VERNE CARUSO • JOHN CASBONA • GIDEON CASHMAN • GIDEON CASHMAN • SAM CASTORO • MICHAEL CATANZARO • CATCH A RISING STAR • CATSKILL HOTELS • GAIL CAUARETTA • GAIL CAVARETTA • DICK CAVETT • BETTY CHAPLIN • SAUL CHAPLIN • RAY CHARLES • CHARLEY O'S • CHEVY CHASE • DESMOND CHILD • BILL CHILDS • CHRISTI • BOB CHRISTIANSON • GEORGE CIHELKA • JOHN CLARK • JILL CLAYBURGH • GEORGE COE • BILL COLE • ED COLE • JAMES COLE, JR. • JAMES COLE, SR. • MATTY COLE • PETER COOK • JOHN COOPER • *THE CORDIAL • ANTHONY CORTINO • ROBERT V. COX • ROBERT V. COX, JR. • MELBOURN CRANSHAW • BRODERICK CRAWFORD • WALTER CRONKITE • MARIA CRUZ • BILLY CRYSTAL • JANE CURTIN • ROY CURTIS • ARTHUR DAHN • RODNEY DANGERFIELD • DANON ON THE PARK • LARRY DAVID • TOM DAVIS • WILLIE DAY • PAUL DE'AK • RICHARD DEAN • LOU DELGATTO • ELLIN DELSENER • RON DELSENER • CAROL DELUISE • DOM DELUISE • STEVE DEMARIA • FRANCOIS DEMENIL • LARRY DEMMLER • ROBERT DEMMLER, JR. • ROBERT DEMMLER, SR. • STEVEN DEMMLER • ALAN DEMKOWICZ • SUE DENIM • LOU DESANTIS • HARIETTE DETJEN • THOMAS DEZENDORF • DIANNE, THE BABYSITTER • DIBBY • THE OLD DICK VAN DYKE SHOW • AUDREY PEART DICKMAN • JOE DICSO • MRS. DICSO • DOUG DILG • PETE DIMOLFETTA • MRS. DIPIETRO • VINCENT DIPIETRO • KIRK DODD • DICK DOHERTY • GEORGE DONOHUE • DOROTHY • KIRK DOUGLAS • JEAN DOUMANIAN • JAMES DOWNEY • BRIAN DOYLE-MURRAY • JANINE DREYER • RICHARD DREYFUSS • MORT DRUCKER • SHELLEY DUVALL • MOSHE AND SUSAN DWORKIN • JANE EASTWOOD • EBBETS FIELD • EDLEN • LARRY EICHLER • ELAINE • ELIZABETH • LOU ELLIS • STEVE EZIAS • KARIN FANTUS • PETER FATOVITCH • DARA FEDER • FRAN ZWEIBEL FEDER • JACLYN FEDER • JESSICA FEDER • RICHIE FEDER • STAN FEIG • ANDREA FEIRSTEIN • BRUCE FEIRSTEIN • GEORGE FEIRSTEN • HELEN FEIRSTEIN • FELDSTEIN'S BUTCHER • JOHN FERGUSON • MARY ALICE FERGUSON • STORM FIELD • CARRIE FISHER • LAURIE FISHMAN • JEFF FITZGERALD • DAVID FLAHERTY • JANE FLAHERTY • JOE FLAHERTY • JUDY FLAHERTY • SHELIA FLATLEY • FOREST LAKE SCHOOL • JOE FORRISTAL • CHERIE FORTIS • JODIE FOSTER • STEPHEN FOSTER • SISTER FRANCESCA • ELLEN FRANK • PATTY FRANK • AL FRANKEN • FRANNIE FRANKEN • THOMASIN FRANKEN • LYNNE FRANKS • BOB FRARACCIO • GARY FRASE • JULIA FRASER • WALT FRAZIER • AUNT FREDA • BOBBY FREUND • NANCY FREY • THE FRIAR'S CLUB • BRUCE J. FRIEDMAN • BUD FRIEDMAN • HAROLD FRIEDMAN • DIANE VON FURSTENBERG • EVAN GALEN • BARBARA GALLAGHER • AL GALLO • FRED GALLO • MIKE GALLO • TOM GAMMIL • VICTOR GARBER • ART GARFUNKEL • TERI GARR • THORNTON GEARY • DUANE GEISZ • GOLDALEE GEISZ • KIM GEISZ • RICK GEISZ • GEORGE'S DELICATESSEN • GEORGE W. HEWLETT HIGH SCHOOL • JOE GILLAM, JR. • JOE GILLAM, SR. • ELIZABETH CLEMENTINE GILLIES • JIM GILLIES • VERNA GILLIES • RUSTY GINZBURG • GIGI GIVERTZ • PAUL GIWOYNA • LARRY GLACY • BOB GLUKLICK • ESTHER GLUKLICK • IRVING GLUKLICK • BILL GROETZ • GOLDSMITH, YAKER & GOLDSMITH • LYNN GOLDSMITH • LENORE GOODMAN • MARTHA GORDON • RUTH GORDON • EYDIE GORME • KATHI GORRINGE • JAN GOSAR • DAVE GOULD • ELLIOTT GOULD • MIKE GOULD • DR. WILBUR GOULD • BARBARA GRABER • BENNY GRAMMATICO • GRANDPA • DIANA GRASSELLI • DAVID GREENWALD • LARRY GREY • JULANN GRIFFIN • CHUCK GRODIN • BILL GROOM • DR. ALAN GROSS • MARGIE GROSS • PENNY GROSS • ROBYN GROSS • TERRY GUARNIERI • ANNA GUEVARA • MIRIAM GUEVARA • MORTY GUNTY • GUYS 'N DOLLS • EDD HALL • CHERYL HARDWICK • MICHELLE HARPER • JAMES HARRIS • GEORGE HARRISON • MR. HART • JOHN HARTY, JR. • RICH HARTY • JOHN HEAD • HUGH HEFNER • AUNT HELEN • BUCK HENRY • CARL HENRY • CARL HENRY, III • JIM HENRY • HOWARD HESSEMAN • GREGORY HINES • DONNA RAE HIRT • JANIS HIRSCH • JAY HOLMAN • HUGH HOLT • THE OLD HOMESTEAD • PAUL HORNUNG • JIM HOSBEIN • JOHN HOWARD • LAUREN HOWARD • WILLIAM HOWARD • LAURIE HUDSON • YVONNE HUDSON • THE HON. STEVE HUFF • THE HUNTINGTON TOWNHOUSE • JOE HUTCHINSON • PAULINE HUTTON • PHIL HYMES • MISSY NORD HAGGARTY • ERIC IDLE • FRANK ILLO • LARRY IMBER • THE IMPROVISATION • UNCLE IRVING • ATTORNEY IRWIN • VICTORIA IRWIN • JUDY JACKLIN • KATE JACKSON • ABE JACOB • JEAN JAMES • PAUL JAMES • JAN • THE JESSE DIXON SINGERS • THE '69 JETS • JOHN JIEMBACK, JR. • HOWARD JOHNSON • DAVE JONAS • BETTY JANE JONES • NORBERTO JONES • MADELINE KAHN • JEROME KALLIMORE • JOSH KANE • VINNIE KANE • STANLEY H. KAPLAN • ELIZABETH KAROLYI • MARGARET KAROLYI • JAN KASOFF • BARBARA KASTNER • FRED KASTNER • KEITH KASTNER • BEN KATSER • MOLLY KATSER • PAM KATZ • KEVIN KAY • JACK KEEGAN • BOB KEESHAN • SHELIA KEHOE • SUSAN KELLERMAN • BARBARA KELLY • CRAIG KELLUM • JEAN KERR • WALTER KERR • JEANNINE KERWIN • WALTER KERWIN • ROBERT KERZMAN • MARGOT KIDDER • ELLEN KIMMEL • ALAN KING • BARBARA ZWEIBEL KIPNIS • DEBORAH KIPNIS • JOEY KIPNIS • STEVEN KIPNIS • MARK KLEIN • MARTY KLEIN • ROY KLEIN • KEVIN KLINE • KENNY KNEITEL • THE '70 KNICKS • TED KNIGHT • MAYOR KOCH • ARNIE KOGEN • FRANCES KOLAR • BARBARA KOLB • JOE KONOPKA • JACK KORNBERG • JIM KOUF • SANDY KOUFAX • KATE KOVACS • RALPH KRAMDEN • CONNIE KRAMER • J. J. KRAMER • KRIS KRISTOPHERSON • NANCY LABREQUE • BETTY LABRETT • PETE LALA • FRANK LARIGNA • LOUISE LASSER • FRANK LAUGHLIN • T. C. LAUGHLIN • JOE LAUER • MITCHELL LAURENCE • STEVE LAWRENCE • DION THE LAWYER • THE LAZO'S • NORMAN LEAR • CAL LEASURE • CHRISTOPHER LEE • EUGENE LEE • FRANNE LEE • LARRY LEE • WILLIE LEE • SID LEINWAND • SID LEINWAND • DAVID LESHAY • DEB LEVY • EUGENE LEVY • FRED LEVY • HENRY LEVY • JOYCE LEVY • JUDY LEVY • LANCE LEVY • NEIL LEVY • PEP LEVY • SARAH LEVY • WENDY LEVY • ARTIE LEWIS • JACK LEWIS • RICHARD LEWIS • BOB LIFTIN • THE LIGGETT SCHOOL • CHRIS LINDNER • MRS. LIPOWITZ • STEVE LISBERGER • BOB LISSNER • THE LITTLE RASCALS • DR. LIVOTI • TED LONG • HECTOR LOPEZ • DICK LORD • UNCA LOU • IRENE LOVE • LUISE • BOB LUMUSCIO • KEN LUPANO • DERMOT LYNCH • TESSIE LYNCH • PATRICK LYNCH • PATTY MACDOUGALL • JOE MACEDA • STEWART MACGREGORY • MADDERLAKE • MADISON SQUARE GARDEN • STANLEY MALIN • TOM MALONE • GEORGE MANOS • MICKEY MANTLE • LOU MARINI • ROGER MARIS • KAY MARK • TONY MARRERO • RUDY MARRONE • SANDRA MARSH • TERRENCE MARSH • PENNY MARSHALL • ANDREA MARTIN • GENE MARTIN • JANE MARTIN • STEVE MARTIN • STRUTHER MARTIN • BEN MASTERS • WALTER MATTHAU • LEE MAYMAN • WILLIE MAYS • IGGY MAXWELL • JIM MAYO • RICHARD MAZANEK • BRUCE MCCALL • JAMES MCCANN • EILEEN MCCOLLUM • BRIAN MCCONNACHIE & FAMILY • CHRISTINA MCGINNESS • FRANK MCGUINESS • JIM MCKEARNAN • DR. MENZES • MERLIN • DOLPH MERTZ • EDWARD METH • THE 1969 METS • LORNE MICHAELS • SUSAN FORRISTAL MICHAELS • ROSIE MICHAELS • MARCUS MILLER • MARILYN SUZANNE MILLER • MITCH MILLER • MINDELL CLEANERS • KATHY MINKOWSKY • BOB MOMUSCIO • EARL MONROE • ANNETTE MOORE • DUDLEY MOORE • MARY MOORE • RICK MORANIS • ROGER MORGAN • HAZEL MORLEY • JAMES MORONI • FRANCESCA MORRIS • GARRETT MORRIS • JOHN MORRIS • RICHARD MORRIS • SENATOR MOYNIHAN • M.T.V. • ROBERT MULHOLLAND • LEON MUNIER • THE MUPPETS • ANDY MURPHY • BILL MURRAY • HOMER BANKS MURRAY • MICKEY MURRAY • LAILA NABULSI • RALPH NADER • BOB NALLAN • JOSEPH NAPOLITANO • UNCLE NAT • DR. ISAAC NELSON • RICK NELSON • RON NESSEN • MATT NEUMAN • TEDDY NEWHALL • BOB NEWHART • LARAINE NEWMAN • RANDY NEWMAN • RICK NEWMAN • JEANNIE NG • NICE STUFF • MIKE NICHOLS • NILS NICHOLS • AL NICOSIA • TOM NOLAN, JR. • TOM NOLAN, III • ED NORTON • DON NOVELLO • KATHY NOVELLO • STEVE NOVICK • PAT O'DONAHUE • MICHAEL O'DONOGHUE • AL OERTER • KATHERINE OGDEN • NICK O'GORMAN • CATHERINE O'HARA • MARCUS O'HARA • PAT O'KEEFE • VICKI OLSON • BOB O'MALLOY • ONE FIFTH AVENUE • OSCAR'S NOSH • EVELYN OSTIN • MO OSTIN • ALBERT PACKARD • RANDY PADGETT • JEAN PAGLUSO • MICHAEL PAHIOS • SARAH PALEY • MICHAEL PALIN • BASIL PAO • DON PARDO • PASTRAMI 'N THINGS • KEVIN PATTERSON • CORINNE PEARLMAN • GIL PEARLMAN • JORDAN PEARLMAN • STEVEN PEARLMAN • ERIC PERGEAUX • KITTY PERGEAUX • ANTHONY PERKINS • PEGGY PETERSON • BILL PETRYK • CARMINE PICIOCCIO • MARK PICK • JENNIFER PINKHAM • KATHY MINKOWSKI PINTARO • JOHN PINTO • PIPS • MARY KAY PLACE • ROBIN PLAVENER • THE POITIERS • THE POLO GROUNDS • KIMBERLY POLSON • BOB POOK • SANDY POUSSAINT • DORIS POWELL • EMILY PRAGER • PAULA PRENTISS • MAX PROSS • PRYOR, CASHMAN, SHERMAN & FLYNN • RICHARD PRYOR • DICK PURUS • QUINCY • LYN QUIYOU • CATHY RADNER • MRS. H. RADNER • HERMAN RADNER • INKY RADNER • JANIE RADNER • MARGIE RADNER • MICHAEL RADNER • NEIL RADNER • RITA RADNER • SPARKLE RADNER • ANNE RAMIS • HAROLD RAMIS • VIOLET RAMIS • PHIL RAMONE • IRENE RAMP • ARTHUR RANKIN • THE RANSAHOFFS • THE RASCHES • RAYMOND • JOE REILLY, JR. • RAY REILLY • CARL REINER • ESTELLE REINER • ROB REINER • THE RESNICKS • RIBS • HERBERT RICE • THE RIGHTEOUS BROTHERS • HEINE RIPP • GERALDO RIVERA • PHIL RIZZUTO • RUTH ROBERTS • DENISE ROBINSON • DR. SOL RODBART • JACK ROLLINS • FREDDY ROMAN • BILL ROMANELLO • ROSA • SUSAN ROSCHELE • DIANE ROSEN • RABBI ROSENBAUM • DR. LARRY ROSENTHAL • DR. LARRY ROSENTHAL • STEVE ROSKIN • LILLIAN ROSS • KAREN ROSTON • HYMAN ROTH • GENE ROWLAND • RAY ROWLAND, JR. • ALAN RUBIN • BILL RUSSELL • RUSTY'S RESTAURANT • TOM RUTLEDGE • HARRY RYAN • BERNIE SAHLENS • JANE SAHLENS • DAVE SALTMAN • ESA SALTMAN • DAVID SANBORN • STACY SANDLER • FRAN SAPERSTEIN • HERB SARGENT • MICHAEL SARRAZIN • SATIN • DON SCARDINO • ROSE ANN SCARMADELLO • TOM SEAVER • HARRY SETON • SUE SETON • DR. SCHEIER • TOM SCHILLER • GEORGE SCHULTZ • HENRY SCHWARTZ • SUSAN SCHWARTZ • NATHAN SCHWARTZ-SALANT • BARRY SECUNDA • NINA SEELY • PAUL SHAFFER • SHAFTAN'S PHARMACY • KAUTHAR SHARIF • SHEA STADIUM • HARRY SHEARER • SUSAN SHEEHAN • JACK SHEEHAN • MARTIN SHEEN • WERNER SHERER • ROBIN SHLIEN • DAVID SHORE • HOWARD SHORE • MAY SHORE • MARTY SHORT • NANCY SHORT • BILL SHORTRIDGE, SR. • AL SIEGAL • PEGGY SIEGAL • JAMES SIGNORELLI • SAMUEL SILBER • MARK SILBERMAN • HARPER SIMON • NEIL SIMON • PAUL SIMON • O. J. SIMPSON • THE SINUKS • BOB SKERRY • DAVID SKLARE • SKULL'S ANGELS • AVIVA SLESIN • CHERYL SLOAN • GERTRUDE SLOAN • JOYCE SLOAN • IRENE SMIRNOFF • BONNIE SUE SMITH • GEORGE EDWARD SMITH • MARLENE SMITH • MAURICIO SMITH • DUKE SNIDER • DR. FREDERIC SNYDER • SOLTERS & ROSKIN • SISSY SPACEK • JOHN SPAGNOLA • BRUCE SPARKS • KAREN SPECHT • JOEL SPECTOR • MISKALL SPILLMAN • STAN SPITZER • LAURI SPOLAN • STAN SPRITZER • PENNY STALLINGS • MAUREEN STAPLETON • RUSTY STAUB • CARL STEIGELBAURER • CLIFF STEIGELBAUER • DAVID STEIGELBAUER • MICHAEL STEIGELBAUER • SAUL STEIN • RICHARD STOCKER • ELIZABETH STONE • THE ROLLING STONES • BAILEY STORTZ • DARRYL STRAWBERRY • HOWARD STRAWBRIDGE • SHIRLEE STROTHER • DAN SULLIVAN • JOHN SULLIVAN • SUNY AT BUFFALO • FRAN TARKENTON • JAMES TAYLOR • THE TEMPTATIONS • ROSALIE TENENBAUM • STEVE TENENBAUM • RABBI TEPLITZ • ROGELIO TERAN • DAVE THOMAS • MICHAEL THOMAS • BILL THOMPSON • JOE THOMPSON • TISCHLER'S • TRISH TODD • LILY TOMLIN • NICK TORITTO • UNIVERSITY OF TORONTO • DEBBIE TRAUM • RICK TRAUM • RICHARD TRUGLIO • GREGORY TULL • DOLLY TURNER • ETHEL TURNER • FRED TURNER • IRWIN TURNER • NANCY TURNER • CICELY TYSON • TRIP ULLRICH • TRIP ULLRICH, III • MIRIAM VALLE • BROOKS VAN HORN • NICK VANOFF • BOB VAN RY • MARIA VIDAL • DR. ISAAC VIDOR • CHARLES VIGILANTE • RAY VOEGE • ED VOSS • GEORGE WADENIUS • MENDY WAGER • GENE WALDSTEIN • JORDON WALKER • VIVIENNE WALKER • WALLY'S • EILEEN WALSH • MATTY WALTZER • RICK WALZER • JANET WARD • GEORGE WASIELKE • SAM WATERSTON • ANNE WEINBLATT • MIKE WEINBLATT • GARY WEIS • DR. GERALD WEISS • ERIC WEISMAN • MARY LOUISE WEISMAN • LIZ WELCH • RACQUEL WELCH • JAN WENNER • JANE WENNER • GEORGETTE WEREMIUK • SANDY WERNICK • JERRY WEXLER • RENE WEXLER • JERRY WHALEN • ERNIE WHITE • ROBERT WHITEHEAD • SIMON WIESENTHAL • GENE WILDER • KATE WILDER • MARY JO WILDER • FRED WILLARD • BUDDY WILLIAMS • CHARLIE WILLIAMS • CINDY WILLIAMS • RALPH WILLIAMS • SYDNEY WILLIAMS • WALTER WILLIAMS • KAY WILMOT • JACK WILNER • DAVE WILSON • ROBERTA WILSON • ANN WINGFIELD • HENRY WINKLER • MARYANN WLOCK • LOU WOKAL • JOY WOOD • WILLIAM WOOD • MAX WRIGHT • PETER WRONGA, JR. • ISAIAH WYMAN • YANKEE STADIUM • THE '61 YANKEES • LEO YOSHIMURA • LINDA YOSHIMURA • ZABAR'S • DON ZAKARIN • EILEEN ZAKARIN • GARY ZAKARIN • MICHAEL ZAKARIN • LAURIE ZAKS • JOE ZALOON • FRANK ZAPPA • ZIMMERMAN • ZINGONE GROCERS • BOB ZOTTERELLI • ADAM ZWEIBEL • BARBARA ZWEIBEL • DUCHESS ZWEIBEL • DUKE ZWEIBEL • FANNY ZWEIBEL • FIFI ZWEIBEL • FRANCINE ZWEIBEL • HYMAN ZWEIBEL • JULIUS ZWEIBEL • LOOPIE ZWEIBEL • ROBIN BLANKMAN ZWEIBEL • SHIRLEY ZWEIBEL • DR. MARVIN ZUCKERMAN • EDDIE ZYNE • SUSAN ZYNE

With extra thanks to Rosie Shuster for hiring the incompetent.

Hey, wanna get thanked? Write your name here ____________

. . . success is 1% inspiration,
95% perspiration, 3% deodorant,
and 1% on your shirt. . . . .

R. R.

Preface

Call me Roseanne Roseannadanna. It all started on October 15th, 1946 in a tiny apartment located above a laundry establishment on Amsterdam Avenue in New York City, New York. My Father, Bert Roseannadanna, Jr., and my Mother, Carlotta Maria Roseanne Roseannadanna, owned and operated The Very Wet Launderette which featured complete laundry services for do-it-yourself-or-you-do-it-for-me-customers.

Laundry had been in the Roseannadanna family for many generations dating to as far back as The Old Country. It was one day, many years ago, when my Nanna (Estelle Roseannadanna) and my Grandfather (Bert Roseannadanna, Sr.) were washing their clothes on some rocks and they figured out that The Old Country was getting so old that they better leave. But, where would they go? What would they pack? Who would they go with? How would they get there? Where was the boat? What if they drown? Isn't it rich? Send in the clowns! Then, they tell me, my Nanna bolted straight up from her rock like she was shot out of a cannon and yelled,

"Hey, Bert! I wanna be in America!"

Bert Sr. was as confused as a horse with a sandwich in its tail! So he yelled back,

"But, Estelle, why do we gotta go there?"

And Nanna yelled back loud and clear with a big Old Country smile on her cute face,

"Everythin' free in America!
I wanna be in America!"

Well, Bert Sr. was no fool. So he calmed Nanna down
and quietly said to her,

> "Okay, by me, in America!
> Everythin' free in America!
> Anythin' goes in America!
> Let's wash these clothes in America!"

So my Grandparents came to The New World with a
lot of damp clothes and some rocks. They were looking
for their golden opportunity and they found it. I should
tell you here that The Roseannadannas were the crispest,
cleanest, tidiest, and cutest little immigrants you ever saw.
It wasn't long before the other scrungy, icky-looking
immigrants were asking my relatives to do their laundry
for them while they were building roads and trying to
think up a government and stuff.

Thus, the Roseannadannas scrubbed, washed, dried,
and folded a lot of immigrant clothes. They worked like a
couple o' dogs and you know what they got for it?
Nothing! Nada! Zilch! Zippo! Zero! Zap! It only took Bert
Sr. a couple of months to get depressed in a way that only
a refugee would understand. One day, he turned to
Nanna and said,

> "Hey! We're gonna starve to death in America!
> How can this be in America?"

And Nanna turned to him with a curious, naturalized
citizen look in her eye and said,

> "But, Bert Sr., everythin' free in America!"

And Bert Sr. yelled back,

> "Is meat free?
> Is chicken free?
> Is oatmeal and milk and sugar free?"

And little Nanna yelled back at him,

> "Hey, don't talk about food.
> I'm so hungry, I could eat my foot!!"

I gotta tell you right here and now that Nanna Roseanna-danna's foot was not exactly the most appetizing foot in the world. It was small and tan and veiny and the pinky toenail curled up and the rest of the foot was all dry and weird and flaky from walking around The Old Country with no shoes on. So, the mere thought of eating one of those things was enough to make my Grandfather bolt out of his chair like he was shot from a canine and bark,

> "Nanna, we're not gonna starve to death in America! You wanna know why?
> Well, I'll tell you why!
> I'm gonna start chargin' money to clean clothes in America!"

Now, this may sound like a pretty obvious idea to you, Mr./Mrs./Ms. Reader, but before you start getting an attitude about my Grandparent's intelligence, you should realize that this was a revolutionary idea for 1904. A lot of those immigrants would rather jump off the pier and swim back to The Old Country than pay for their laundry. Fortunately, Bert Sr. had the Roseannadanna gift o' gab and he was able to calm the wretched refuse. He just explained to them that America was the land of free enterprise which meant that immigrants like them were *not* free to work for free in America, but they *were* free to be free to be you and me in America. And those huddled masses bought it! Or at least they said they knew what he was talking about, anyway.

Anyways, I don't have to tell you that after that brainstorm, Nanna and Bert Sr. had enough nickels, dimes, and quarters to drown a small pope. Why, they even got confident enough to move their entire washing establishment including the night watchman out of their 33rd floor tenement walk-up and to open up The Very

Wet Launderette on the corner of 96th Street and Amsterdam Avenue on the West Side of New York City. Who would believe it? It was The American Dream come true. The Roseannadannas now had their own business and their own apartment!

But, my Grandfather was confused. Never before in the history of my family did anyone live in one place and do their work in another place. How was he gonna do both? He got so depressed that he didn't get out of bed for about nine days because he really thought he'd spread himself too thin. Nanna kept telling him that he was being too hard on himself and he should get out of bed 'cause the sheets were starting to smell like New Jersey. And then in the middle of the night, out of nowhere, my Grandfather sat up in bed and said,

> "Estelle, I figured it out!
> I can commute!"

But Estelle didn't hear him because by this time she was sleeping on the couch 'cause she couldn't take the stench in the bedroom. So, at breakfast, when Bert Sr. told her his new revolutionary idea, she said that he better hurry up or else he'd be late for work and they both had a good laugh over that one.

Well, needless to say, it was clear sailing from there. The Very Wet Lauderette was a tribute to clean clothes and Roseannadanna ingenuity and it flourished and progressed just like America did. When the washing machine got invented, the Roseannadannas got one. When the dryer got invented, the Roseannadannas got one of those too. When the coin-operated washer and dryer got invented, my Grandfather couldn't figure out how to attach the coin part to his old machines so he decided to have a baby. He said to Nanna,

> "That way, when I die (God-forbid, knock-wood, bite your tongue, pick your face) there'll be someone to inherit the store so the Roseannadannas won't be . . . and try to forget I'm

sayin' this . . . 'washed-up' in the laundry business."

Nanna agreed.

So in 1921, Estelle and Bert Roseannadanna, Sr. gave birth to my Father, Bert Roseannadanna, Jr. He was a smart boy who took to laundry like a hair takes to soap and he was thrilled as a pig in a blanket to be in the family business. As a matter of fact, he was obsessed with it. When he was growing up and all his little friends were out playing refugee games like "Curse The Czar!" or "Hit the Pickle," Bert Jr. would be inside The Very Wet Launderette telling the night watchman that "spinning," "tumbling," and "cycling" were not only the words he wanted on his tattoo, but were also the traits that he wanted in a wife. And everyday, the night watchman would look at the starry-eyed, optimistic, full of hopes 'n dreams Bert Roseannadanna, Jr., and say to him,

"Hey, if I'm a night watchman, how come I'm here in the afternoon?"

Now, my Mother's name was Carlotta Maria Roseanne Bobaria (you pronouce it Beau-Ba-Ree-Yah as in Di-Ah-Ree-Ah) and she spinned and tumbled and cycled into my Father's life in the summer of 1942. Carlotta was the only daughter of Roseanne Maria and Bo Bobaria and everynight she would spin and tumble and twist and fly aroun' 'n aroun' in the air with her parents while everyone cheered and applauded below. Yes, it's true, if you haven't already guessed, I, Roseanne Roseannadanna, am descended from "the Flying Bobarias," which is probably why I have a natural flair for show business and a snappy way about me. It must be because of the circus in the blood of a laundryman's daughter. Now, I'll tell you how that all happened.

Every night, my Father would put on his best suit and go to the circus to watch the lovely and talented Carlotta Maria Roseanne Bobaria (pronounced Boe-Bar-Ree-Yah) as she was passed back and forth in midair between

Roseanne Maria and Bo Bobaria. It was something to see! Years later, my romantic Father said that his heart used to beat so hard he thought he was gonna rip his nipple. He was so in love he couldn't sleep at night and he started writing a diary. He said he wouldn't mind if I showed you a page from it in this book:

Sunday, June 12th

Dear Diary,

Imagine me, Bert Roseannadanna Jr., being married to Carlotta Marie Roseanne Bobaria (Pronounced 🎀 + 👥👥 + 🌳 − T + AH)

Naw, it couldn't happen. She's with the circus. She's like a rolling stone. She's a gypsy. She's a tramp. She's a theif. She's a ½ breed. She's sunny. She's cheerful. She's a rebel and she'll never be any good. But I love her so. And I'm gonna make her love me. Yes, I will. Yes, I will. 'Cause baby, I need your lovin'. So, hold on, I'm comin'. I got you, babe. I believe in magic. We're happy together. You're havin' my baby. It's a boy named Sue. Hey, you don't send me no flowers. You lost that lovin' feelin' Baby, baby, where did our love go? We can work it out. Breaking up is hard to do. There goes my baby. I'm a loser. I'm all shook up. I'm havin' my nineteenth nervous breakdown.

Time is not on my side. It's a rainy day. It's Monday. This is getting me down. I'm gonna cry ninety-six tears. It's impossible.
Help!

But, my Father, Bert Roseannadanna, Jr., the laun-
derer, didn't give up! He decided to ask Carlotta Maria
Roseanne Bobaria, the trapeze artist, to marry him. And
why not? As anyone in the laundry business knows:

> "Life is like a busted washing machine,
> You only go around once!"

So he proposed to Carlotta Maria Roseanne Bobaria and
waited for her to say, "yes."

Then, it happened! On this one night, my Father was
sitting under the Big Top watching Carlotta Maria
Roseanne Bobaria and her parents, Roseanne Maria and
Bo Bobaria perform their most dangerous and death-
defying feat. I never saw this death-defying feat, but they
say it had a lot of spinning and tumbling and twisting by
my Mother and hopefully a lot of catching by my Grandparents in it. They only did this feat once a night and I'm
told that everytime they did it, the crowd was so quiet you
could hear the elephants sitting.

Anyways, something went wrong that particular night.
My Grandfather said years later that he had a little tickle in
his ear. He said it was the kind that goes so deep you try
to scratch it with your tongue on the inside of your mouth.
He said he was swinging by his feet and the tongue-
scratch wasn't working so he had to use his pinky finger to
really get deep in there. When it was his turn to catch my
Mother, he couldn't keep up his end of the deal 'cause his
pinky finger was inside of his ear shaking so fast it looked
like a little hummingbird's wings. So, my Mother, Carlotta
Maria R. Bobaria, started falling from high atop the Big
Top and my Father and everyone else held their breath as
she screamed at the top of her big lungs,

> "I only want three things!
> One . . . I want to land in the net!
> Two . . . I hope there's peace in the world!
> Three . . . If I do land in the net, I want my
> name to be:
> Carlotta Maria Roseanne Bobaria Roseanna-
> danna, Jr."

THE ROSEANNADANNAS

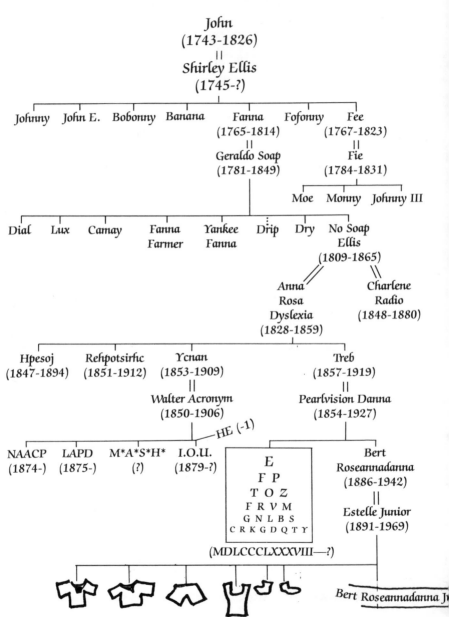

THE BOBARIAS

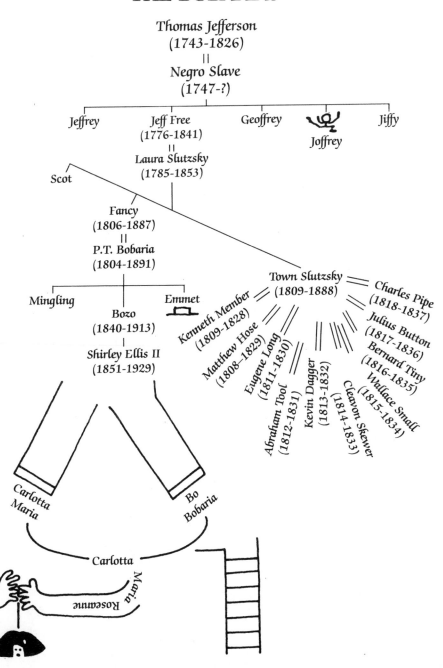

Well, I'm not gonna leave you in suspense any longer. My Mother landed in the net and bounced around a couple of times and then crawled out of the net and took a bow. Needless to say, the crowd cheered, the clowns danced, the popcorn popped, the seals barked, the peanuts peed, the bearded lady shaved, and my Father, Bert Roseannadanna, Jr. was so happy he thought he was gonna die! But, he didn't die (Thank-God, Amen, Praise the Lord, Break the Wind) and they got married exactly seven minutes before I was conceived which says a lot about the Roseannadanna timing.

My Mother worked right through her pregnancy until she got too heavy to catch and then she left the circus forever to live above The Very Wet Launderette and be the lovely wife of Bert Roseannadanna, Jr. Business was going very well, but with the new tiny baby coming and my Grandparents commuting, my Father worried about money and his future in dirty clothes. But every Roseannadanna knows a new baby brings good fortune and my extraordinary birth was no exception.

It was the night of October 15, 1946 and my Mother, Carlotta Maria (you know the rest of her name by now) started feeling something weird going on inside of her. She said it kinda felt like her stomach was eating a lemon or something and it was all scrunched up and wanted to spit the lemon out. Well, my Father didn't have to be hit over the head with an obstetrician to know that this meant the little tiny-baby-me was gonna come out. He called a taxi to take them to the hospital, but the taxi-people said it would be a twenty to a hundred and twenty minute wait or more. But, my Father didn't panic. He figured out that my Mother was getting these pains "about the time it takes to tumble dry a cotton blanket" apart from each other. So he made my Mother all nice and comfortable on the kitchen table and told her not to worry and to take deep breaths and be patient and when the pains started coming every "about the time it takes to tumble dry a handkerchief" that he was gonna roll up his sleeves and deliver the cute little baby himself unless the taxi came, but it didn't. So, he did.

And oh what a darling little baby I was! I saw a picture. I was a doll—a beautiful, no blood or creamy white stuff on my face, living doll! I came out as spanking clean and tidy as anything that had ever been washed at my Father's launderette. The only messy part was this one little teeny-tiny red/yellow/blue/green sorta wet dot that flew out of my Mother's you-know-what and landed on my Father's favorite sweater. I don't remember any of this even though that dot-thing came out after I was already out. My Father says he put me on my Mother's belly and I was rollin' aroun' 'n aroun' on there while he was tryin' everything to get that red/yellow/blue/green dot-blotch off his sweater. He tried soap. He tried water. He tried soap and water. He spit on the dot and tried to rub it out with his finger.

But no matter how much he picked it and scraped it and washed it, that little red/yellow/blue/green dot just wouldn't come out. That's when my Father, Bert Roseannadanna, Jr., looked at my Mother and me lying on the kitchen table and said,

> "This is it! This is the sign we've been waitin' for!
>
> We're gonna be rich and we're gonna be able to commute just like my parents!
>
> And you know how we're gonna do that?
>
> We're gonna open a brand new dry cleaning establishment so I can get this disgusting dot-blotch off my sweater!"

EDITOR'S NOTE: I find it necessary to interrupt the text in order to inform the Reader that we at Long Shadow Books gave Ms. Roseannadanna a huge advance to write a book about coping with the unemployment problem. It was not our intention to finance her autobiography and it is our hope that Ms. Roseannadanna will keep this in mind and get to the point soon.

And so it came to pass and was true and really did happen and all that stuff. My parents named me Roseanne after my maternal Grandmother, Roseanne Maria Bobaria, and right after I was born, my Father opened The Very Dry Dry Cleaners on Columbus Avenue and 92nd Street. Us three Roseannadannas still lived above The Very Wet Launderette and commuted the five blocks to The Very Dry Dry Cleaners. We were very comfortable and had lots o' money 'cause my Father worked like a dog.

I loved growing up in The Very Dry Dry Cleaners 'cause it was always so warm and cozy and dry and I'll never forget this little sign that my Father hung on the wall. It was the kind of personal touch my Father gave his customers that made him into the success that he was. He was a little embarrassed about it, but he said I could show it to you in my book:

WARNING:

THE DRY-CLEANING
GENERAL HAS
DETERMINED THAT
TEETH THAT ARE
CHIPPED WHEN YOU
TRY TO REMOVE
THE STAPLES FROM
YOUR SHIRTS
PROBABLY WEREN'T
IN THAT GOOD A
SHAPE TO BEGIN
WITH.

HAVE A DRY DRY DAY!

B.R.J.

And so, the business and my family prospered because my Father was nobody's fool. And let's face it, even if he was somebody's fool, nobody could think of who that somebody was so everybody walked around saying that if there was anybody who was nobody's fool it probably was my Father. Just to show you what I mean I'm gonna tell you this thing that happened to me when I was a little girl and had just started going to school. This is a pretty long story so I'm gonna start a new paragraph. It'll look better.

Every morning, my Father and my Mother used to take turns dressing me and making sure I always looked clean and fresh so that all the other kids at school would like me and not make fun of me or anything like they did about Hernando Roseannadando. Hernando was this kid in my class that no one ever wanted to sit next to in the cafeteria 'cause his lunch always smelled the way I figure the inside of Neil Armstrong's spacesuit smelled like after he got back from the moon. Anyways, this one day I was sitting with my little classmates in the cafeteria and eating this delicious peanut butter sandwich my Mother and Father had stayed up the whole night before making for me and I was drinking my milk out of this cute little container that was like the kind you collect pennies for UNICEF in. We were all laughing and giggling like there's no tomorrow 'cause Hernando was eating the same exact lunch that he always ate: two hard-boiled eggs, a mashed potato sandwich, a green pepper, and a bag of bar-b-qued potato chips,

So, we were laughing our guts out at Hernando and I was talking and laughing so much and eating at the same time that all of a sudden the milk that I was drinking started coming out of my nose. I couldn't believe it! There I was just sitting there with all of this milk shooting out of me. I didn't know what to do! I didn't even know that your mouth and your nose were connected to each other on the inside! Then, everyone in the cafeteria started looking at me and when they saw what was happening on my face with milk coming out of my nose holes, they went nuts! They just forgot about Hernando Roseannadando and started laughing at me, the little Roseanne Roseannadanna. And the more they laughed, the more milk came shooting out. I didn't know there was that much milk in the carton! They started to yell,

"Hey, Roseanne, what are ya? A fountain?"

"Hey, Roseanne, your nose is lactating!"

"Hey, Roseanne, why don't you jump up 'n down 'n spin aroun' so we can all have a milkshake!"

And then, as if that wasn't enough, they all stood up and started snappin' their fingers and dancing around the cafeteria like they were in some cheap kid's production of "West Side Story" and they started singing this song to the tune of "When You're A Jet":

When you're a jerk
Milk shoots out of your nose
From the first time you laugh
Milk's all over your clothes!

I was so embarrassed I thought I was gonna die. And then, out of nowhere, these little pieces of my peanut butter sandwich started coming out with the milk and everybody stopped dancing and yelled,

"Hey, Roseanne, enough is enough. What are you trying to do? Make us sick!"

Well, when I got home from school that day, my Father saw that my eyes were all red and puffy from crying and when I told him what happened he said,

"Is that all?
That's no big deal!
That happens to everyone!"

And, to prove his point, that night when he tucked me into bed and made sure I was all cozy and sweet and nice and tiny and snug as a bug in a rug and put powder under my arms and everything, my Father, Bert Jr., told me this little fable that was first told to him by my great Aunt, a woman who was regarded as the matriarch of our family, Carlotta Maria Rose Kennedy Bobaria, and it went like this:

Once upon a time, there was this little parakeet that was depressed as a bird 'cause he had no ears. He worried and worried all day long,

> "What if someone calls me?   ·
> What am I gonna use to keep my glasses up?
> What do I put earmuffs on?
> How'm I gonna wear a hearing aid?
> Where'm I gonna have my earaches?
> What if the Walkman gets invented?
> What am I gonna do with these Q-tips?"

Then, this one day, someone passed the little parakeet a note that said that a bunch of other parakeets were coming into town and the little parakeet that is the hero of this story thought and thought,

> "How'm I gonna face those other parakeets if I don't got ears?
> I can't read lips and even if I could read lips, what do I do if they talk behind my back?
> Why would they talk behind my back?
> What did I do?
> I didn't shoot no one!
> Sure, I got no ears, but is that any reason to be cruel to another bird of a feather?
> I thought we were supposed to stick together!"

Well, this little parakeet got himself so upset about not having ears that he chirped a suicide note to his secretary who started crying 'cause she didn't want her boss to die 'cause then she'd be out o' work. Well, between you and me, Roseanne Roseannadanna, I couldn't take too much more of this story. So, I said to my Father,

> "Hey, Dad Jr., what's this stupid fable got to do with me and the milk that came outta my nose?"

And, my Father said back to me,

> "Well, Roseanne, it just goes to show you, it's always something. If it's not one thing, it's another. Either your friends make you cry at school 'cause you got milk comin' outta your nose, or your own flesh and blood Father tells you a fable that's so stupid you wish you were an orphan. It's just like a little joke I once heard that was written by your Mother's joke-writing first cousin who's gonna be on *The Dick Van Dyke Show,* Carlotta Maria Rose Marie Bobaria, and it went like this:

>> A minister, a rabbi, and a priest walk into a bar and the bartender says,

>>> "Excuse me, men o' the cloth, but I couldn't help but notice that the three of you have milk shooting out of your noses. How come?"

>> So, the minister says,

>>> "I drank milk and started to laugh."

>> And the priest says,

>>> "I just thank God that I don't have a chalice shooting out of my nose."

>> So, the bartender looks at the rabbi and says,

>>> "How 'bout you?"

And the rabbi shook his head and said,

"Nothing could be worse."

And then he started to cry.

"Oh, you're just looking for sympathy,"

said the mean bartender. And with that he threw the rabbi out of the bar into a dark alley where he beat him with one of those long spoons that you mix martinis with. But no one came to help the rabbi 'cause no one was around to hear him crying except for this one little parakeet who was hiding in the alley 'cause some other parakeets were expected in town that day. But when he saw what was happening to the rabbi, the little parakeet started laughing so hard that milk came shooting out of his nose.

Good-night, my little Roseanne Roseannadanna."

EDITOR'S NOTE: The book that we commissioned Ms. Roseannadanna to do was to be an inexpensive, easy-to-read, "non-book" that the Reader can find piled next to the cash register in any book, stationery, or magazine store. We admit that these "non-books" are faddish and add absolutely nothing to the world of literature. But, if we'd wanted art, we would've commissioned Lillian Hellman to write a "Hey, get back to work" book. I assure you, personally, that I will do everything in my power to get this book STARTED. Thank you for your understanding.

So that's the kinda guy my Father was and I knew that when I grew up I was gonna follow in his same-day-service footsteps and go into the dry cleaning business. You better bet, nothing could have made him happier. I remember those afternoons when we'd go for these real long walks up and down the stairs in The Empire State Building and we'd make dry-cleaning plans for the future. We'd talk about how if the good Lord would shine His Roseannadanna smile upon us, we could branch out to the suburbs and open The Very Dry Drive-In Dry Cleaners which is the ultimate dream of all dry-cleaners 'cause both the owners and the customers get the chance to commute!

Anyways, these were our dreams and plans until Lady Luck stepped in and changed the course of my life as well as the course of my future which, of course, are exactly the same courses except that one is a course of a different color. (I don't mind saying myself that that last sentence was beautiful and a bit out o' the ordinary for this kind of book.) Lemme explain. Lady Luck was the name of my guidance counselor at "The Give The Little Lady A Drink And Put It On My Bert Jr. High School" which was located on Columbus Avenue downtown from The Very Dry Dry Cleaners. So, this one day, the telephone rang in our apartment above The Very Wet Launderette and it was Ms. Lady Luck and she told my Father she wanted to meet with him to discuss how his name got to be in the name of the High School and what the results were of the aptitude test I'd taken to find out what I could be when I grew up.

Well, I don't have to tell you how me and my Father stayed up that whole night all scared and crying and holding on to each other and praying our hearts out that I didn't have any talent for anything but dry-cleaning. Bert Roseannadanna Sr. and Bert Roseannadanna Jr. had always prided themselves that neither of them were cut out to do anything else but tend to the business of cleaning things that people got dirty. But, now, my Father and I were faced with the possibility that this trait could (God-forbid, knock on wood, smack your puppy) skip a generation. We were scared as a couple of rabbits with an athlete's foot hanging from their key-chain.

And we were still scared and crying and holding each other and praying that next fateful day in Ms. Lady Luck's office when she looked up at us from her desk and said,

> "LOUD!
> All of her tests indicate that your daughter is LOUD. Roseanne ranks in the 99th percentile when it comes to volume, audibility, projection, decibel levels, shrieking, yelling, screaming, and gashrying. Congratulations, Mr. Roseanna-danna, your daughter is one of the LOUDEST young women in America."

My Father and I were so shocked we stopped praying and crying. Talk about irony! We both figured out that I probably got so loud from learning to talk over all the steaming and shushing and clanking and buzzing and stuff at The Very Dry Dry Cleaners. And now, I would have to leave dry-cleaning behind and go on to a louder calling. I mean I wasn't just loud. I was in the 99th percentile of loud. For crying out loud, that's loud! What was I gonna do??? Would I have to leave dry-cleaning? Would I be the one to end the Roseannadanna clean clothes-line? I couldn't face it. But, as usual, my Father, Bert Roseannadanna, Jr., knew we had to be strong about this new weird quirk of events and to prove his point he stood right up in front of Ms. Lady Luck and he bowed and he took his shirt out of the back of his pants so he looked like he was wearing a tuxedo with tails and he started to sing an inspirational aria that was first made famous by my opera-singing Aunt Carlotta Maria Callas Roseanne Bobaria. But, Ms. Luck told him to tuck his shirt back into his pants and keep his voice down 'cause it was disturbing the other students.

So, me and my Father left "The Give The Little Lady A Drink And Put It On My Bert Jr. High School" and walked back to The Very Dry Dry Cleaners crying and praying and wishing and hoping and thinking and praying and planning and dreaming that maybe my Mother

(CMRBR, Jr.) could give us some advice. But when we got to The Very Dry Dry Cleaners, my Mother said she was sorry, but she couldn't give us any advice 'cause we didn't have a ticket, but if we waited thirty days and no one else came in with the same problem she'd be happy to talk to us about it.

So, me and my Father went back out walking on the streets of New York when who do we see but this out 'n out bum who asks us if we have a match. Well, I was almost positive my Father was gonna say, "Your breath and a buffalo's foot" because this bum did kind of smell like he stepped in something brown. Hey, while we're on the subject, did you ever smell something weird in the house and you look all around in every room to find where it was and then it turns out to be on you? Like your breath got stale or you ate cheese with your fingers or you have on somebody else's sweater. You know, a lotta people don't know this, but your belly button sweats and sometimes you forget to clean it even though you cleaned everything else pretty good. Hey, editor! Did that ever happen to you?

EDITOR'S NOTE: Excuse me?

Did your belly button ever sweat so much that it made a wet smelly circle on your undershirt?

EDITOR'S NOTE: We, at Long Shadow Books, feel this issue has absolutely nothing to do with unemployment.

Hey! Why don't you get off your high editorial horse!

EDITOR'S NOTE: All right. All right. On occasion, I have perspired in or about the navel area. I do work in the city and I do wear a suit so I have to be particularly careful in the dog days of August. Now, Ms. Roseannadanna, can you please . . .

Anyways, me and my father didn't have a match 'cause everyone knows there's never been any member of my family except maybe for my sickly Cousin, Carlotta Maria Roseanne Emphyzema, that ever smoked any cigarette. So, we just kept walking and walking 'till we saw this rhyming-bum who asked us,

> "Excuse me, sir
> And gal so fair,
> But do you have
> A butt to spare?"

When we said we didn't have any cigarettes, this rhyming-bum guy got real mad and bummed out and dropped his pants and threw a book of matches at us and bent over and yelled,

> "Well, here's a butt
> And I don't mean maybe,
> So strike a match
> And light this baby!"

Well, my Father picked the book of matches right off the sidewalk and we ran away as fast as we could. We figured we'd take the matches back to that other bum that had the cigarette 'cause that's the Roseannadanna way. And it was right then that we got the sign we were looking, waiting, hoping, and praying for. On this book of matches was an advertisement for The Columbia Broadcasting School (CBS) which in no way is affiliated with The Columbia Broadcasting System (CBS) or The Colorado School for the Blind (CSB). No matter what, it's still a terrific school and not just anyone can get into it 'cause you gotta pass this real hard test which was right there on the inside of the matchbook. I stuck it on the next page:

IF YOU CAN PASS THIS TEST THEN YOU TOO COULD BE A BROADCAST JOURNALIST

1. TAKE ONE OF THESE MATCHES AND LIGHT IT.

2. NOW, TAKE THE END THAT'S ON FIRE AND TOUCH YOUR PINKY WITH IT.

3. SAY, "OUCH!"

HOW DID YOU SAY "OUCH!"

1.	WERE YOU LOUD?	YES	NO
2.	DID YOU ENUNCIATE?	YES	NO
3.	DID YOU SMILE?	YES	NO
4.	DID YOU SAY IT WITH CREDIBILITY?	YES	NO
5.	COULD YOU SAY IT SITTING BEHIND A DESK?	YES	NO
6.	COULD YOU SAY IT WITH A WEATHERMAN STANDING BEHIND YOU?	YES	NO
7.	COULD YOU SAY IT AT 6:00 AND AGAIN AT 11:00?	YES	NO

Now I don't wanna brag, but I, Roseanne Roseannadanna, was able to answer "YES" to all of those ques-
tions. My Father and me were so happy we would've bet
the family jewels that we were gonna die. My loud
aptitude had found a home and I was gonna be the first
Roseannadanna to go to college.

Well, I can't, so I won't, even try to tell you how my
family gave me this party the night before I started school
and how we sang and danced aroun' 'n aroun' 'n aroun'
all through the night and how when the party was all over
the Roseannadannas and whoever was left of "The
Flying Bobarias" put my suitcase and trunks into the car
and drove me out to the airport where we kissed 'n
hugged 'n said "good-by" 'n waved "good-by" 'n cried
'n cried our little eyes out 'till my loving Father, Bert
Roseannadanna, Jr., took me in his arms and with tears in
his eyes he said,

> "My little Roseanne Roseannadanna,
> It's time for you to go to college and make
> something clean and loud out of yourself.
> I don't want you to be late, so let's
> quit cryin' 'n huggin' and drive back
> 'cause your college is in the city.

So we packed the car all up again and my whole entire
family drove me to my first day at The Columbia Broadcasting School.

College was a snap! I don't think it's possible that I'll
ever forget how when I first got there they made us stand
up and put one hand on our hearts and our other hand
on the flag and say real loud and clear,

EDITOR'S NOTE: I hope it's not another poem.

I pledge allegiance
      'Cause I'm no fool
That's how I got
      Into this school.

I'm so thrilled,
      I want to scream
I wish we had
      A football team.

CBS students are
      A special breed.
I wish we had
      Some books to read.

I want to broadcast
      About world affairs,
I wish we had
      Some desks and chairs.

So get a job
      And be a winner
I'll see you at the
      Alumni dinner.

The Alumni dinner
      Could be real good,
But they won't be serving
      Any food.

So Long!

Well, when I got home from college, my parents were still cleaning the apartment from my going-away party, but as soon as they saw me we started cryin' 'n huggin' 'n kissin' again 'cause now I was the first Roseannadanna to be a college graduate. So they called the whole family up and we started the party all over again. But as we were all driving back out to the airport, I couldn't help but feel in my heart that there was still some more I had to learn about broadcast journalism. No way am I mocking my Alma Mater, mind you. The hour I spent at The Columbia Broadcasting School means a lot to me and I'll always cherish those memories as only a Roseannadanna canna. But what I'm saying is that you can't teach experience and that's what I needed. It's like a Catch-22. It's hard to get experience if you don't got a job and it's hard to get a job if you don't got an interview and I must've gone to a thousand of those job interviews but I got turned down at every single one. I was depressed as a dog, but everytime I got disappointed I'd remember the Roseannadanna philosophy that says that you shouldn't cry over spilt milk 'cause if you spill some milk and instead of cleaning it up you just walk over it and start crying, they're gonna put you on lithium.

EDITOR'S NOTE: I wish I had some lithium . . .

Anyways, I didn't give up. Then, this one rainy day, I was walking up Fifth Avenue making my way to the place where I catch the crosstown bus, when I saw this man in a very smart three-piece suit jumping up and down and cursing his brains out in front of The Sherry Netherland's Hotel. I might add here that The Sherry Netherland's is a very classy hotel with fancy awnings 'n a revolving door 'n a uniformed revolving doorman 'n everything. Well, I'm no prude, but this cursing guy was going nuts. I've never heard disgusting stuff like that before in my life. So, I turned to this sailor who was blushing and I asked him,

"Hey, what's with this guy?"

And the sailor says back,

> "Don't you recognize him?
> That's David Brinkley!"

And it was! It was actually Mr. News-Guy, David Brinkley himself, standing right there in front of The Sherry Netherland's Hotel, swearing like a dockworker! I couldn't believe it! It seems this taxi cab had come zooming by real close to the curb and splashed a puddle that had rain and mud and foam and oil and cigarette butts and horse urine and gum and other New York street goop in it all over the three-piece suit that Brinkley was gonna wear on the news that night. Between you and me, R. R., it looked like he'd been crawling on the sidewalk or something. I didn't even want to think about what else might have been in that puddle and now was all over Dave. Anyways, he's still yellin' and cursin' his head off, so I yell,

> "Hey, David Brinkley!
> Do you kiss your mother with that
> mouth????"

And he yells back,

> "Who are you?"

I yelled back,

> "I'm Roseanne Roseannadanna and I
> just happen to be the daughter of
> the owner of the finest dry-cleaning
> establishment in New York City!"

Well, talk about being in the right place at the right time. Mr. Brinkley actually came with me on the crosstown bus to The Very Dry Dry Cleaners. He was still real p.o.'ed, but when my Father, Bert Roseannadanna, Jr., said to him,

"Strip down, trenchmouth!"

Mr. Brinkley knew my Father meant business and that's exactly what Mr. NBC Nightly News did while me and my Father got all the presses going to clean that three-piece mess before he went on the air.

You woulda loved it! There he was, Mr. David Brinkley, standing in the middle of The Very Dry Dry Cleaners stripped down to his bikini underwear that said "Home Of The Whopper" on the front. He was signing autographs for all our regular customers and also for all the people coming out of The Very Hard Hardware Store and The What A Great Lunch Luncheonette. Then, before you knew it, a crowd started gathering and all the traffic on Columbus Avenue stopped and people started looking out of their car windows and into our store window and they were whistlin' 'n yellin' stuff like:

"Great legs, Dave!"

and

"Sorry about Chet."

and

"What's the news tonight, Brinks?"

and

"That's no Whopper, that's
a filet o' fish!!!"

Well, I can't even tell you about how nuts it was getting out there. This was really the very first celebrity we'd had almost naked in The Very Dry Dry Cleaners. (Though it was to come to be a pretty regular sight in the years to come, but I'll tell you about that later and I know you'll get a big kick out of it if you-know-who doesn't edit it out.)

Then, all of a sudden, my Father comes rushing from the back of the store chanting like he was shot out of a cantor,

> "I can't do it!
> I just can't do it!
> I *can* get the goop outta the
> jacket and the vest and the shirt
> and the tie, but I can't get
> this splotch outta the pants!"

Now, I should tell you I grew up hearing the words: goop, blotch, spot, splotch, soot, yuck, ooze, grease, ick, and gucky a lot. They came UP a lot in the dry-cleaning business, but the most important thing to any dry-cleaner is that they come OUT, and my Father, Bert Roseannadanna, Jr., just couldn't get the splotch outta the pants. He thought he was gonna dye. He didn't want anyone, and especially Mr. Network News, to think he was a bad dry-cleaner (God-forbid, perish the thought, bite your tongue, snap your log). I gotta tell you right now that that splotch on Mr. Brinkley's pants was not from a puddle. It was definitely a splotch from a ball-point pen. He had one in his pocket that had leaked and oozed out into his pocket lining and then made a mess on the front of his good pants which also explained why Davey's fingers were all blue when all this time we figured he had a circulation problem.

Now, I'm getting to the crucial part of this story. There's Mr. David Brinkley and my Father cryin' 'n cryin' over these blotched up pair o' pants and I know that I, Roseanne Roseannadanna, have gotta do something before Brinkley starts swearing again and before my Father puts his head in the martinizing machine. So, I said,

"Hey, Newsman Brinkley!
Wake up and smell the coffee!
You know when you do the news your
legs are under a desk, so
you never needed any pants in the
first place.
Drop the pants all together, Dave!
You could save a fortune on suits!"

Well, I must admit that sometimes I even surprise myself when some of these snappy ideas just ooze outta me 'cause Brinkley started to smile and then his smile got bigger and bigger and then he started clapping and laughing and so did everyone in The Very Dry Dry Cleaners and all the people in their cars and buses and trucks on Columbus Avenue were smilin' 'n clappin' 'n laughin.' Well, Mr. 7:00 News was so happy, I thought he was gonna call Chet. He said that I was a little doll, and he started to give me a hug, but I wouldn't let him 'cause I didn't want that Whopper to turn into a Double-Whopper. I just shook his blue-inky hand and I noticed that he had a teeny, tiny, grateful tear in his eyes when he looked at me and said,

"Thank you, Roseanne Roseannadanna.
I just can't thank you enough for
your intelligence and insight. If
there's ever anything I can do to help
you, please don't hesitate for one
second to get in touch with me."

So, I looked him straight in the eyes and said,

"Hey, Brinkley, remember that
favor you promised me less than one second
ago?"

He said,

"I think so."

Now, I took my little diploma from The Columbia Broad-casting School out of my pocket and held it up and said,

> "The irony of this whole
> thing is that I'm in your
> line of work and I need a
> break!
> Let's face it, when you
> were in trouble, I was there!"

With that, Mr. Brinkley took my hand and we both kissed my parents good-by and ran out into the traffic which formed a big motorcade that took the two of us right down Columbus Avenue (which, as you may or may not know, was named after the ship that my three explorer cousins, Nina, Pinta, and Santa Maria Bobaria sailed in when they were searching for an Avenue). And this motorcade took us all the way downtown where I began my first day of work at NBC.

EDITOR'S NOTE: Roseanne . . .

Well, there it was 1976. I was 363 months old and I was happier than a peacock in third place to be part of the NBC News Department. You shoulda seen me! Every morning I'd leave my little apartment that was still above The Very Wet Launderette and take the bus to the NBC News Department offices that were located in the very beautiful Rockefeller Center. You know the place with the skating rink and the big Christmas tree lighting. Every morning, the elevator operator, Nelson (no relation) would take me up to the sixth floor where this lady named Happy (no relation) would help me change into my cute little NBC news outfit and then I'd go into the newsroom where Oysters (a third cousin) would tell me what my duties were for the day. I was what they called a GOFFER (pronounced go-fer as in go-fer-stuff). And that's exactly what I did. I went for stuff. Like if Hugh Downs needed some pipe tobacco or if Linda Ellerbee needed some moustache bleach or if Jane Curtin needed someone to go down to the pier and unload her crate of Modess every month, I was the one who did it. And lunchtime was a very big time for me. I mean everybody wants lunch and I was the perfect person to go-fer it. Lemme just show you a few of the orders I filled in my first days at NBC:

Jane Pauley
watercress finger sandwich
herbal tea
Tom Brokaw
*same as Barbara W
Marv Albert
wheat germ on alfalfa
sprouts
Lloyd Dobbins
buck wheat on alfalfa
sprouts
Dick Schapp
Spanky on alfalfa
sprouts.

John Chancellor
head-cheese on rye + a diet
mountain dew.
David Brinkley
double cheese whopper / no
cheese.
Barbara Walters
roasted leg'o lamb on bed
'o lettuce with lots'o relish
1/2 pint light 'n lively
yogurt + a little bit 'o
lemon
Gene Shalit
beef barley soup
a straw and a
catcher's mask.

So, anyways, I was always runnin' aroun' 'n aroun' and when I wasn't I was hangin' aroun' 'n aroun' trying to learn as much as I could about broadcast journalism. I especially liked hangin' aroun' the teletype machines so that I could see those fast-breaking stories as they came tickin' over the wire and then I'd hand 'em to the newscaster so they could read 'em on the air. It was thrilling. You know, a lot of people don't know this, but not all the news goes on the air. There are big meetings and stuff to see what stories go on and what stories we could live without. It all depends on how much news there is and how much time there is and everything. Between you and me, Roseanne Roseannadanna, I don't think I'll ever forget this one meeting where Chancellor said he didn't think it was necessary to report the 1976 Presidential Election returns and he put up a big stink about it, but everyone else vetoed him. Well, it's a good think he didn't get his way 'cause ABC and CBS covered the election and if we didn't we woulda looked stupid.

Well, I worked real hard at NBC News and after about a year or so I became, if I do say so myself, and why shouldn't I, I might ask, if you please, a very important cog in the NBC News Wheel. If anyone needed something, the big joke 'roun' the newsroom was "Roseanne knows where it's at!" Well, everyone used to sit aroun' laughing their fast-breaking faces off at that joke which is really a pretty funny joke although I imagine it's probably a lot funnier if you're a broadcast journalist at NBC. But, this one particular night, the joke was on me! I should say here that this is the first time I'm revealing this story publicly, but this is my book and this is my story like it was. So get all cozy and snug and turn on the lamp and let's go for some interesting stuff I never told anyone.

EDITOR'S NOTE: Roseanne . . . .

It was in December of 1976 and I was working the night shift. It was about three o'clock in the morning and we were getting ready to sign off the air. Jessica Savitch had just finished the final news wrap-up and now the NBC minister was on the air reciting a good-night psalm. All of a sudden, Walter Celery, the NBC vice-president in charge of sign-offs, came running into the newsroom screaming like a Banshee that he couldn't find the film clip of "The Star-Spangled Banner." He said that they had the picture of the test pattern and they had the film clip of all the static, but "The Star-Spangled Banner" was nowhere to be found. So when he asked if any of us knew where it was, everyone that was still left in the newsroom at that hour looked up and said in unison,

"Roseanne knows where it's at!"

And then they all started laughing. Well, of course, I knew exactly where it was at, but I couldn't tell Mr. Celery 'cause I didn't want to get anyone in trouble. You see, earlier that day, Beverly Sills had stopped by the news-room and said that she was supposed to sing the national anthem at Madison's Square Gardens for the opening game of The Stanley Cup Playoffs and she wanted to bone up on the words and the music of "The Star-Spangled Banner." Anyways, someone on the morning shift lent her the clip and now the problem was that "Bubbles" still hadn't returned it 'cause she went out partying with The Rangers after the game. The NBC minister was now reciting himself 'til he was blue in the countenance with his twelfth psalm trying to stall for more time. Meanwhile, I was pretending to look real hard for the clip while secretly thinking it was probably floating in some punchbowl somewhere. What a journalistic di-lemma! Do I snitch on Beverly and expose the fact that one of our greatest opera singers was out high-sticking with a hockey team? Or do I keep my mouth shut and risk NBC getting in trouble with The Federal Communica-tions Commission? You see, the FCC has a law that says if you don't end your programming day with "The Star-Spangled Banner" you have to move the whole network to Russia.

EDITOR'S NOTE: *Wait a minute. I've never heard of such
a . . . Roseanne . . .*

It wasn't what you'd call a pretty sight with everyone in
that newsroom rifling through file cabinets and lookin' in
drawers and cryin' because they didn't want to live
behind The Iron Curtain, while in the studio, the NBC
minister had just finished reciting all the psalms and was
now showing some photographs of his family. Then, all of
a sudden, back in the newsroom, I, Roseanne Roseannadanna, surprised even myself, R_2, when I grabbed a small
thin slice of bread and jumped on to a desk like I was shot
out of a canapé and yelled,

"I can do it!"

Well, that stopped everyone right in their tracks and they
just stayed frozen like that until someone asked,

"You can do what?"

And I said,

"I can do "The Star-Spangled Banner.""

Then, they all froze again until Walter Celery, the vice-
president of sign-offs, asked,

"What makes you qualified?"

Well, I can't even begin to describe the applause and the
commotion that went on when I whipped out my diploma
from The Columbia Broadcasting School so I won't even
try. Let's just say that once again I was in the right place at
the right time. My fellow cohorts were so relieved and
excited that they hoisted me up onto their shoulders and
carried me to the set where the NBC minister was now
doing card tricks and where I was gonna sing and act out
"The Star-Spangled Banner."

Now, let me set the record straight about something. Ordinarily, when I, Roseanne Roseannadanna, sing a song, I sound just like a cute little lark. It's a beautiful thing to hear. But, as I'm sure you all know, when it comes to "The Star-Spangled Banner" even the most professional singers have trouble with it. Not only are the lyrics hard to remember, but musically, it's a real difficult tune to carry aroun'. Like if perchance you should start on a note that's just a little bit too high (God-forbid, perish the thought, bite your lip, sell your car) by the time you get to the middle of song, you're in big trouble. Like I figure I was nervous and I must've started on too high a note 'cause by the time I got to the "and the rockets red glare" part, you never heard such a high-pitched sound in your life. They tell me I hit a frequency that was really up there 'cause the RCA dog started barking, the lights on the Rockefeller Christmas Tree started flashing, and as if that wasn't enough, NBC got its highest ratings in 6 years 'cause TV sets that were turned off all of a sudden went on by themselves. It was 4:00 in the morning and millions of sleepers were awakened by the sound of me, Roseanne Roseannadanna, singing "The Star-Spangled Banner" on TV.

Well, the rest, as the saying goes, is television history. The network was flooded with so many phone calls that The NBC exceutives offered me my own variety special. I turned it down. I was a newswoman and in the news was where I wanted to stay! And, obviously, that's where you, Mr./Mrs./Ms./M.P.H. Viewer/Reader wanted me to stay 'cause your mail said so.

On the next page, I'm reprinting a typical sample of the many letters that deluged NBC after my first national appearance singing "The Star-Spangled Banner."

It all happened so fast it coulda made your head counselor spin! Before you knew it, there I was flyin' aroun' from here to there, meetin' this one, interviewin' that one, breakin' the news, makin' the news, and (like when I broke the story about the The Hite Report) orgasmically fakin' the news. NBC had me workin' like a

Richard Feder
Fort Lee, New Jersey
December 28, 1976

Dear Roseanne Roseannnnnadannnnna —

Hey, who are you? How did you get on T.V.?
Is it hard to get on T.V.? Can I get on T.V.?
Can you fix my T.V.? Can you fix the mirror in
my medicine cabinet? They both broke when I saw
you on T.V. last night.

Which reminds me. Last night, when you
sang that song you said that we watched RAMPARTS!
Hey, what are **RAMPARTS?** That's the only line of
the song that you didn't act out. How come? I
know what a ram is. I also know what parts are.
So, if I put them together does it mean a ram's
parts? A ram's private parts? . . . . Oh, I get it.
That's why you couldn't act it out on T.V. ... But let
me ask you something else then ... When all
those rockets had a red glare and all those bombs
were bursting in air, how come we all just
stood around looking at what was underneath
a ram? Someone coulda gotten killed!

Sincerely yours,
Richard Feder

P.S. Just in case you feel bad about ruining
that song. Don't! Earlier last night other I
went to a hockey game and Beverly Sills
sang that same song and cracked the ice.

hot-dog in heat. I was tired, but I loved every minute of it. And why shouldn't I love it, may I ask? I was quite the gal. You might even say I was "the Toast of The Town" or, if I might say it, I'd say I was "The Toast o' the Town," "The Belle o' the Ball," and "The Apple o' Every Optician's Eye!" My face was my ticket! Every place that it was important to be at, I WAS! And every place I WAS became important to be at! Jimmy Carter used to love to tell people that Sadat and Begin and him coulda reached an accord on the mideast problem months before they did if they hadn't decided to put their meeting off 'til I was in the vicinity of Camp David. Although, between you and me, R(R), I wish they would've gone ahead without me because Camp David was one of the most disgusting experiences I've ever had. Anwar kept on getting those nosebleeds from the high altitude and even though Menachim and I begged him to use a handkerchief, Sadat must've thought that that was a threat to his Middle Eastern masculinity 'cause he kept saying,

> "The West Bank, I'll talk to you about. But, when it comes to my nose, that's my business!"

And he insisted on using his shirt cuffs to soak up the blood and his fingers to try to stop the bleeding. Not only was I, Roseanne Roseannadanna, never made so sick by an Egyptian before, but it also made Begin and Carter sick. That's why they kept passing all those pens back 'n forth 'n everythin' when they were signing the treaty 'cause they all had little pieces of dried-up blood on 'em and so did the treaty.

Anyways, those years were fast and zippy and like everyone who's "The Toast o' The Town," I kept all my clippings in a scrapbook so I could look back on them when I was old and show them to my Roseannagrand-children. That was before I knew I was gonna write this book so I figure I'll show them to you now so you can get a real grasp of the magnitude of my career.

EDITOR'S NOTE: Scrapbook?

THE WEST SIDE TV SHOPPER

AND RESTAURANT GUIDE

Jan. 1, 1977

FREE

Roseanne Roseannadanna
Dry-Cleaner's Daughter Hits High Note
Page 17

Manhattan Restaurant Index
Page 58-59

Bruce Sinclair reviews
The Front Porch & La Reserve
Page 41

d was "dishonest be-
nd things that were
objective facts out of
. As a piece of litera-
tact. If I were teach-

woman whose gums I care about is my ——
ter when she comes home from the orthodon-
tist." Former Democratic Party chairman Robert Strauss, a good friend of Allen's, also puts
in his two cents, describing Allen as "the least

deals. People are saying, 'I didn't know y
were that tough or that mean' ... I have no respect for McClintock, but I appreciate him as
a deal finder."

PAGE SIX

HALSTON: RR to R$_x$

What makes for a bad night of
boogying? Ask Studio 54 regular, De-
signer Halston. "I'm just happy that
Newswoman, Roseanne Roseanna-

danna, had a bandaid with her when
my Italian Gucci loafers were caus-
ing me to raise a blister on the heel
of my foot." Says Roseanne, "Hey, I always carry a box 'o mixed bandaids
wherever I go. You gotta have a variety. Like what if someone bursts a little pimple ... then you gotta have a
spot-shaped one for that 'n those tiny
strips are for paper cuts on your finger, but that Halston needed a big
long fat thick bandaid 'cause he had

a real mess there on his heel. There
was blood 'n puss 'n clear wet stuff
'n little black threads from his socks
where the skin broke. It was makin'
me so sick I had to ask Liza Minnelli
to sing "New York, New York" just to
get my mind off it."

Discovered

THOUGH   artist   Theodoros
Stamos f———

Barry Goldwater blocks son's rival

CONSE———VE Sen. Barry Goldwater isn't on the Senate Foreign
Relations ———

'S
onetime
—— been

SSSh!

it's a Surprise Party

FOR _Bella Abzug_
BY _Bess Myerson_
AT _Polly Bergen's_
R.S.V.P. _Marlo Thomas_

Bring Yourself

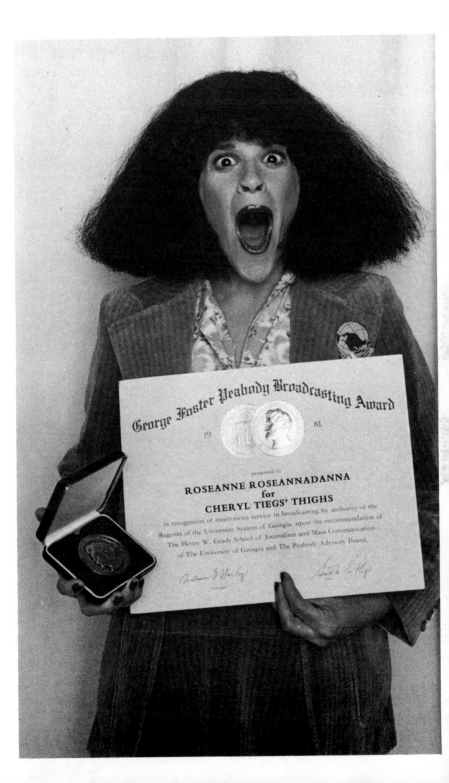

THE CITY OF NEW YORK
OFFICE OF THE MAYOR
NEW YORK, N.Y. 10007

June 28

Dear Roseanne,

Thank you for stopping by the mansion for lunch. What a surprise! Oh, my staff and I were wondering if you left a handkerchief with the monogram R.R. in the ladies room. If it's yours, we'll wash it and send it out. If it isn't yours... please let us know so we can give Rex Reed a call.

Sincerely,

Ed

Ed

P.S. I enjoyed your five part series. More!

TONIGHT ✦ NBC
10:00

HEY, WHAT GIVES!

Roseanne Roseannadanna spends an intimate hour with David Frost discussing his televised interviews with Richard Nixon which she missed because her T.V. was stolen.

4N

WATCH TONIGHT!
RR AND DAVID FROST

Milestones

RECOVERING, Carlotta Maria Rose-anne Bobaria (acrobatic mother of television's Roseanne Roseannadanna) from a broken nose, a broken jaw, and multiple facial lacerations when the curtain rod she was hanging upside down from gave way when she was voting.

ILL. Mamie Eisenhower, 82, widow of President Dwight D. Eisenhower, after suffering a stroke in her Gettysburg, Pa., home and being rushed to Walter Reed Army Medical Center in Washington, D.C. Frail and bedridden for several months, the former First Lady is reported to have "some loss of function" in her right side and difficulty forming sentences.

ILL. Rose Kennedy, 89, matriarch of the Kennedy clan; after undergoing surgery to repair an intestinal hernia; in Boston. "The operation went well," her physician reported. "She's a tough old gal. She was swimming just two days ago."

DIED, Gracie Fields, sassy English chanteuse and actress who started as a shilling-a-week trouper in working men's cl.

ale

LIZ SMITH

ff

ess shifts.
n easy-care

7-12.57

ff

umbrellas,
s, more.
7.77

ff

partment.
l shoulder
more.
1.17

Dragging it.

Reporting it.

"No. I wasn't invited to Woody's New Year's Eve party," **Roseanne Roseannadanna** told me. "It's his loss. That party'll be like 'o funeral without me." Seems that **Princess Lee Radziwell** is still fuming over Roseanne's reporting on network T.V. that she had a long strip of toilet paper dragging from her shoe when she recently emerged from the ladies' room in **Elaine's** and Woody is siding with the Princess. **Mia Farrow** says that her steady cherishes his own privacy and can understand why Ms. Radziwell is angry. Is Roseanne upset about spending New Year's Eve alone? "Hell no! Just where is she the Princess of, anyways?"

To ROSEANNE ROSEANNADANNA
Date JULY 8   Time 10:45 A.M./P.M.
WHILE YOU WERE OUT
MS. DIANE VON FURSTENBERG
of _____
Area Code
& Exchange _____

TELEPHONED	☒	PLEASE CALL	
CALLED TO SEE YOU		WILL CALL AGAIN	
WANTS TO SEE YOU		URGENT	
	RETURNED YOUR CALL		

Message YOU COULD
SMELL BETTER.

_____ Operator

DOONESBURY
by Garry Trudeau

THE GLOBAL NEWSPAPER
Edited in Paris
Printed Simultaneously in
Paris, London, Zurich,
Hong Kong and Singapore

WEATHER DATA APPEAR ON PAGE 14

Herald INTERNATIONAL Trib

Published With The New York Times and The Washington Post

PARIS, TUESDAY, APRIL 19, 19.

***

No. 31,152

MAO DEAD? "No way," claims American Newswoman, Roseanne Roseannadanna, who traveled halfway around the world to refute the rumor. "Not only is this Mao guy alive," reports Roseannadanna, "But from the bubbles I could see comin' up from his bathing suit, I figure Mr. Chairman has enough life in him to carbonate the Yangtse."

Walesa Detained by Polish Police

Habib ar.
continuing
Mr. Hab
in the presi
(eight kilom
of the explo:
wife, Robert;
NBC televisi
embassy at t
sion and he r;
to search for
said she was
with cuts on t
Mr. Dillon
Gemayel an
Shafiq al-Waz
expressed sho
over the blas
do," he said,
this stop our w
Of his own
lon said: "I wa
telephone in c
shirt in the ot
jogging, when
office collapsed
Mr. Dillon s;
could not move
"Then the s
pieces of rubb
me," he contin
of a broken wi
floors and out."
The blast, a
time, brought d
central wing of
blew a large
ground floor v
northern wing.
An Associate
said the center
ground to the ro
layer cake and
seen dangling fr
Two other wi
were still standi
sustained heavy
Witnesses said

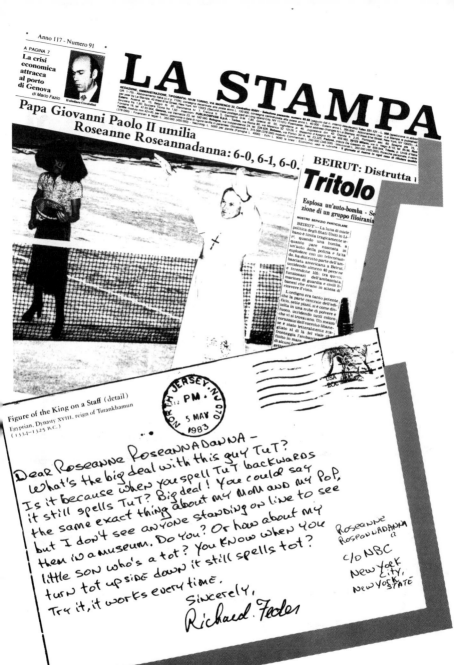

Ryan's Hope

No, Ryan O'Neal, 37, is not showing Roseanne Roseannadanna, 31, how good he was in "Love Story" with Ali McGraw, 39. What Tatum's dad is pointing to are the photogs that were snapping pictures of R. ("Hey, What Gives?") R. and him as they were leaving his luxurious east side pad. "Can't a man have his shirt cleaned in peace?" Ryan snapped back before he and R_2 got into his limo to go out for a sandwich." Sure. But how did he lose those buttons on his shirt? And why didn't they go to Roseanne's pad above The Very Wet Launderette? Was "the Main Event" just a "Paper Moon," or is Ryan Lyin' ???????

Fat City>

If patrons of the fashionable Ma Maison restaurant in

RANDOM NOTES

When Roseanne Rose-annadanna showed up at New York Lone Star Cafe last Friday night, it was as an audience member. The popular newscaster in town after a recent trip to Iran, came to see Ronstadt perform. "She's good. She takes my mind off of stuff," said Roseanne. But when introduced to the audience by Linda herself, the excited crowd made it difficult for Roseanne not to go up and join Linda in a rendition of "Desperado." Said Roseanne afterwards, "It felt good. It took my mind off of stuff."

Ronstadt and Roseannadanna closed the Lone Star

Strutting beneath a Picasso-esque set and wearing

say I should find out soon") and home computers ("I got into show

After the show, patrons headed for a fancy-pants party at Club A,

The Presidential Inaugural Committee
requests the honor of your presence
to attend and participate in the Inauguration of

Ronald Wilson Reagan

as President of the United States of America

and

George Herbert Walker Bush

as Vice President of the United States of America
on Tuesday the twentieth of January
one thousand nine hundred and eighty one
in the City of Washington

That's the way it was. And to this very day whenever I'm driving across The George Washington Bridge or going through The Mary Todd Lincoln Tunnel, it isn't unusual for all of the toll collectors to get off their seats, step outside, jump up on top of their booths, put their arms around each other, start precision kicking like the Rockettes, and shout in unison at the top of their cute little Transit Authority lungs,

"Hey, Roseanne Roseannadanna, of all the things you experienced as a Hotshot Newswoman, what would you say was your biggest thrill?"

So, I always pull over to the side of the road and wait for all the dancing toll collectors to get off work and when they do I sit them down in a circle and tell them that without a doubt the most memorable and thrilling moment in my snappy career had to be President Ronald Reagan's Inauguration.

EDITOR'S NOTE: I have reached the point where I need some help.

PUBLISHER'S NOTE: What's the problem?

EDITOR'S NOTE: I'm sorry to bother you, sir, but Ms. Roseannadanna appears to be out of control and I don't know how to deal with her.

PUBLISHER'S NOTE: Out of control? Fire her!

EDITOR'S NOTE: Roseanne?

ROSEANNE'S NOTE: What?

EDITOR'S NOTE: You're fired!

ROSEANNE'S NOTE: Hey, that's real funny . . .

Anyways, where was I? Oh! The Inauguration! Yeah. It was January 20, 1981.

EDITOR'S NOTE: Sorry to disturb you again, sir . . .

PUBLISHER'S NOTE: What now?

EDITOR'S NOTE: Ms. Roseannadanna appears to refuse to acknowledge the fact that we have fired her.

PUBLISHER'S NOTE: What do you mean she appears to refuse to acknowledge the fact that we have fired her? Don't you know that an Editor is supposed to . . . ?

EDITOR'S NOTE: But, sir . . .

PUBLISHER'S NOTE: Don't interrupt. Not only do you appear to be a vascillating milquetoast, but you're also rude. You're fired!

Anyways, January 20, 1981 . . .

EDITOR'S NOTE: Roseanne?

ROSEANNE'S NOTE: What now, Ed.?

EDITOR'S NOTE: I lost my job. What should I do?

ROSEANNE'S NOTE: Buy this book!

So, January 20, 1981 was a real zippy and patriotic time for the whole country. Everyone was full of all kinds of new hope that a new leader would give us a new beginning and make us all feel happy and new again. And why shouldn't we feel that way? We deserved it! We'd been through a lot and it was time for a transition o' power. It's just like any political scientist will tell you:

> "America is like a little teeny tiny baby who wears a diaper . . . If you don't change it periodically, a lot of stuff builds up that might eventually hit the fan."

So, January 20, 1981 was a great time for a celebration and a perfect day for it too. The skies were clear and it was a perky 56°. America had just gotten the news that Iran had finally released our hostages (Thank-God, Hallaluyah, cross your heart, tip your waiter) and they were on their way home. But, I think that I, Roseanne Roseannadanna, was the happiest American of all. I was assigned to cover The Inauguration and I can only tell you that what might of been just another day's work was, for me, a labor o' love. You see, I always had a secret crush on Ronald Reagan all the way back to his "Death Valley" days. And who could blame me? He was big. He was strong. He was handsome. And I'd be lying to you if I didn't say he got my adolescent juices flowing and set my Roseannadanimagination on fire. I used to sit in all my classes daydreaming about Ron and doodling in my looseleaf. I saved all my looseleafs so I'll show you a typical page:

$$\heartsuit(R^2) + \heartsuit(R^2) = \heartsuit(2R^2) \nearrow \text{ECSTASY}$$

$$R^2 \times R^2 = R^4 \qquad \frac{R^2}{R^2}$$

$$\sqrt{\frac{R^2}{R^4}}$$

Roseanne Rosannareagan
Roseanne Reagadanna

$$+\ \frac{\begin{array}{l} 2\ young \\ 2\ go \end{array}}{4\ Ron} \qquad\qquad +\ \frac{\begin{array}{l} 2\ old \\ 2\ run \end{array}}{4\ mesidant}$$

And now my childhood dreamboat was about to become President of The United States of America. I truly believed he was just the guy we needed for America's recovery. So I guess you can imagine how upset I was when right in the middle of Reagan's inaugural address, Rosalynn Carter turned to me and whispered that just before they left, she and Jimmy put saran wrap over all the toilet bowls in the White House. Well, I thought I was gonna slap her face off! How dare they do that! What kind of respect is that for our new administration's first excretions and vice-excretions? But, I decided not to make a big thing out of it 'cause I didn't want to interrupt Ronald during his speech. I just turned a cold Roseannadanna shoulder to that sore-loser-sour-puss from Plains and made a mental note to bring a hunting knife with me the next time I had to use the Ladies' room in The White House.

After The Inauguration, I went back to my hotel room and spent the rest of the day gettin' myself all dolled up for The Inaugural Ball. Talk about "steppin' out!" This bash made Prince Charles 'n Lady Di's wedding seem like "Fish-Fry Night" at Ho Jo's! All of D'n C was aglow with lights and tinsel and glitter and movie stars that Reagan knew from the olden days. All 'n all, there were ten different balls all over the city. Each one had their own guest list and their own big band entertainment. But those of us in the know knew that anybody who was anybody was at the ball that was in The Kennedy Center. The Frank Sinatras, The Johnny Carsons, The Bob Hopes, The Liz Taylors, The Bill Blass', The Kirk Douglas', The Hugh O'Briens, The Jimmy Stewarts, The Alexander Haigs, The Henry Kissingers, The Walter Annenbergs, as well as Alfred and Betsy Bloomingdale were there. And I, The Roseanne Roseannadanna, was there too. Although, I must admit that I was a little p.o.'ed when I found out that I was seated at the singles' table with Muriel Humphrey, Lady Bird Johnson, Bess Truman, Alf Landon, General Omar Bradley, Helen Hayes, Mamie Eisenhower, and The President's ballet-dancing son, Ron. But I figured it was a great honor just to be a part of all this hoopla so I didn't make a big thing about it.

Hey, I know you're dying to know what I, R.R., wore to this extravaganza ball. All I can say is I was dressed to the hilt! I wore one of these long, beaded, diaphanous Adolpho evening gowns. It was a strapless one with kind of like metal slats coming up from the waist inside to keep it straight up on my body. Lemme tell you, the top part of that dress never moved once. No matter what I did with my arms and shoulders that top part stayed there like the Iron Curtain. It was a little tiny bit tight and I had one of those push-up brassiere-rigs in it so that I was pushed-up in the front enough to show that I'm really quite the gal, but not so much that General Bradley'd think the war was still on and this was a USO Tour or anything. Everybody else was dressed in their inaugural best too and I fit right in. The men had on black ties and tuxedoes and the women had on their fanciest, smanciest Adolpho or Bill Blass or James Galanos or Oscar de LaRenta gowns except for Liz Taylor who wore a gown that must've been by Barnum and/or Bailey. Personally, I would like to take this opportunity to mention that I chose my gown out of a rack of clothes that nobody had picked up for over six months at The Very Dry Dry Cleaners.

At The Kennedy Center Ball, they had Les Brown's Band O' Renown playing and an open bar where everyone stood aroun' cracking jokes like,

"What Table are you at?"

and

"Fritz Mondale called . . . Collect!"

and

"What's the difference between a Jewish American Princess and George Bush?"

I never did find out the answer to that riddle 'cause I spent most of my time hangin' around the lavish buffet hors d'oeuvre table. It was pretty interesting to see how everybody was trying their famished best to eat as much as they could while they were also trying their diplomatic best to not look like a bunch o' pigs. Well, Mr./Mrs./Ms./DDS. Reader, just between you and me, Roseanne Roseannadanna, you wouldn't believe the way these hotsy totsies eat at a Ball. Like Lorne Green was there and he'd load up two plates of this fancy chow mein stuff and then tell the guy that was dishing it out that one of the plates was for Hoss. And Esteé Lauder kept saying that the cute little hot dogs wrapped in tiny jackets smelled so good that she just had to bottle the fragrance and then she dumped about ninety of them into her purse. Kirk Douglas was even hiding little potato puffs in his chin. And, listen to this, The Reverend Billy Graham actually brought his own toothpick. It was shaped like a little cross with tiny strips of colored cellophane on the end and when he didn't think anyone was looking, he'd whip it out and stab a melon ball and eat it. He was also using that crosspick thing to get shrimps and then he'd stash 'em in his vest pocket. I guess that was in case he didn't like the main course.

I should tell you, I was having my own troubles at that hors d'oeuvre table. You see, I was eating these cracked crab claws like they were going out of style. They were delicious and chewy, but what I realized was that the Government forgot to put out a bowl or a tray or something to put the shells in when you were done eating the crab part. This was like a $500-a-plate hoity-toity Ball with no place for garbage. There I was in my Inaugural diaphanous Adolpho gown standing aroun' with a pile of empty cracked crab claw shells in my hand. I didn't know what to do with them. At first, I was thinking about flippin' them back on to the smorgasbord, but just then William and Pat Buckley walked by and I was afraid they'd see me. Then I thought about sticking them down the front of my diaphanous Adolpho gown, but there wasn't room for anything else in there. I finally figured out that I'd just start gently dropping them one at a time on the floor while making my way to the Ladies' room, but just as I started on my way, Ms. Katherine Graham grabbed my arm and said the Reagans were just about to open their gifts. So, I very politely wrapped the shells inside a linen napkin with a presidential seal on it and brought it back to the singles' table with me.

The Reagans got a lot of potted plants and Cuisinarts for their new house. There were a lot of duplications, but I figure they got enough staff to do the returning and exchanging. Dinner was:

FRUIT CUP
CHICKEN CONSOMME
TOSSED GREEN SALAD

CHOICE OF
PRIME RIBS AU JUS
or

CORNISH HEN

COFFEE
VIENNESE TABLE

In case you don't know, a Viennese table is where you can make your own sundaes. And just let me say that the minute they rolled that table out, everyone bolted from their seats and rushed towards it like they were a bunch o' horses running in The Kentucky Derby. Everyone was pushin' 'n shovin' 'n jockeyin' for a good position at the table. It was a bloodbath! Betsy Bloomingdale got her front tooth chipped by Nancy Kissinger's bracelet when they were both goin' for the whipped cream. Alexander Haig kept stabbing people in their hands with a spoon and saying, "I'm in charge here" whenever they tried to get to the chopped nuts. And even The Rev. Billy Graham was up to his old tricks when he took out his crucifix-toothpick and stole everyone's marachino cherries when they weren't looking.

Afterwards, everyone was so full that they loosened their belts, undid the tops of their pants, and just sat back and enjoyed the sounds of Lou Rawls, Tony Bennett, and Dennis Day. I really enjoy Lou Rawls and Tony Bennett, but I've always had a special thing going for Dennis Day since I was a little girl. I used to dream about how I, Roseanne Roseannadanna, would marry Dennis Day and then my name could be R_2D_2. So, now, I also leaned back in my chair and closed my eyes and listened blissfully to Dennis singing the theme to The Jack Benny Show. It was wonderful. I felt so peaceful and serene and calm. Although, I gotta admit that feeling calm wasn't too difficult a way to feel considering the wax museum of a table they had me sitting at. I mean these weren't exactly a bunch o' live wires. The only talking going on at the table was Ron, the President's son. He was sitting right next to me and he kept saying,

> "I hope they don't make me dance. I hope they don't make me dance. Everytime my parents have a party, they embarrass me by making me dance. I hope they don't make me dance."

Well, this guy kept sayin' the same thing over and over again like he was a broken record or something. But, he obviously knew what he was talkin' about 'cause when The First Lady and The President came over to be in our table photograph, Nancy leaned down and sweetly asked Ron if he'd be a good boy and dance for everyone. Well, I guess you know by now that Ron-boy wasn't too thrilled to hear this, but when First Lady Nancy started cryin' and said that Ron never gave her any pleasure, just aggravation, and when she started to wave all the bills for his dancing lessons in his face, Ron said,

> "Okay . . . Okay!"

and left the table to go change into his tights.

Well, I always try not to get myself involved in other people's family arguments, but I was kinda glad that Ron was gonna dance. I'd heard that he was pretty good and, who knew, this might be a good break for him with all those show-biz people there. I got all excited when they made the ballroom dark and there was a kind of hush all over the room. The orchestra played a nifty overture and then a spotlight appeared on Ron as he came out onstage to dance the guy's part in "Swan Lake." Now, lemme say here that Ron looked great! His hair was all slicked back. His posture was terrific. He had on a little red short jacket and gray tights and he looked just like Barishnikov or Nureyev or Gudunov or any of those other Russian defectors who dance aroun' looking like they're smuggling bottles of Stolichnaya in the front of their tights. Did you ever see those guys? I don't think I've ever even looked at their faces! Just what have they got in there anyway? That couldn't be all them! I always figure they keep an extra pair of toeshoes in there! I mean if those things grow like that in Russia, we could get involved in a whole other kind of missiles race with the Soviets. I do know that they all wear this cup aroun' that part to support and protect it from other things and itself while they're dancing. At least I know that Nureyev does and Barishnikov does and Alvin Ailey does, but that night little Ron Reagan didn't. You see, when he stood up on his tiptoes and started walking across the stage, this crunching sound came out of his crotch. The more he walked, the more it crunched. I couldn't believe it! When he did a plié, his crotch-crunched. When he did a relevé, his crotch-crunched. And when he glided across the stage and jumped up and landed in a split, not only were there lots o' crunches, but he started yelling. Then Ron popped right up and was spinnin' and yellin' and spinnin' and yellin' and even though I don't know that much about ballet, I had a feeling that somethin' was really wrong. At this point, Ron was holding on to his crunching-crotch and spinnin' and turnin' and yellin' and I didn't think that I had ever seen that in "Swan Lake" before.

I must say here that it got a little painful to watch even though Ron was doing his best and it was his parents' party and everything. I had to lower my eyes and just pretend I was watching. So, I was looking down at the table for just a second when what do I see, but this supporter-protector cup with a Presidential Seal on it lying right next to where my napkin with all the cracked crab claw shells in it used to be. Well, that explained where all that crunching was coming from. It was bad enough that Ron picked up that napkin by mistake, but you can imagine how nervous he must've been not to notice that he was stuffing his tights with cracked crab claw shells. I yanked one of the metal wires out of my diaphanous Adolpho and pierced the cup and held it out and yelled,

"Hey, Ron, you forgot this!"

But it was too late. Everyone in the place was on their feet clappin' and applaudin' and shoutin' "Bravo!" and the orchestra was playin' faster and faster tryin' to keep up with Ron who was now spinnin' 'n twirlin' faster than all of my Father's washers and dryers put together. What else could I do except go along with everyone when they joined hands and formed a circle and started dancing around The First Family's spinnin' son.

Afterwards, everyone thanked the Reagans for inviting them and said it was the best Inaugural Ball they'd ever been to. President Reagan begged everybody to take some food home with them 'cause there was plenty left over and he didn't want to let it go to waste, but we were all too full then to think we might be hungry later. The Rev. Billy Graham was the only one who took him up on it and said,

"Okay . . . Maybe I'll take a few melon balls."

As for dancing Ron, he did okay for himself that night. Whatever damage he did inside his tights cleared up enough for him to get married and he also got a job dancing professionally for The Joffrey Ballet which is a pretty fancy and respectable company. Come to think about it, he did a lot better than a lotta other people did 'cause soon after his father took office, millions of Americans, including me, Roseanne Roseannadanna, found themselves out o' work.

Hey, this book is turning out to be pretty heavy stuff, huh? I bet that you Readers got so caught up in all that great party excitement that that last sentence took you by surprise. Well, you can imagine how I felt! I was shocked as a fish that got caught by an electrician. But let me unfold for you what happened.

So, January 21, 1981, the day after the Inauguration, I took the shuttle from Washington D 'n C back to New York City. It was just a regular airplane shuttle, not the shuttle like the astronauts use. But you wanna know something? I was in such a terrific post-inaugural mood that I was wishin' I could take that other space shuttle. Then, I woulda got to go to Cape Canaveral, blast off, circle the earth for three or four days, land somewhere in the desert, go through a bunch o' medical tests, get some fresh clothes, and then take a real plane from wherever I landed back to New York City. Now, that woulda given me a lot more time to think about what a lucky gal I was. A gal who grew up on top of a launderette and turned into a "somebody" at the top of her profession. A gal who just spent time with her childhood fantasy flame on the biggest day of his life. Hey, it was pretty much the biggest day of my life too! And all of our lives! 'Cause as I sat there on that shuttle, still wearing my strapless, beaded, diaphanous Adolpho gown from the night before, I truly believed that our country, The U.S.'o A. was on the verge of somethin' real snappy and that things were gonna be exciting 'n romantic again. It was gonna be like "Camelot!" No, wait a minute. I just remembered that The Kennedy Years were just like "Camelot." Okay, then it would be just like "Hello Dolly!" That's it! No. I just remembered that Madison's administration was called The "Hello Dolly" Years. Well, then it would be like

"Thieves!" No. "Thieves" were The Nixon Years. What about "Oh! Cal . . . ." no, those were The Coolidge Years.

Anyways, I was sure I would've come up with what kind of years it'd be if I'd taken that other shuttle. But when this shuttle landed at La Guardia (the airport that the Mayor was named after), I was still in such a cele-breagan mood that it didn't even register when a sky-cap said,

> "Sorry about what happened, Ms. Roseanna-danna."

as he was helping me into a taxi-cab. So I just smiled at him as the taxi-cab pulled away and started towards the city. At first, I thought I'd go back to my apartment above The Very Wet Launderette so I could change out of my strapless, beaded, diaphanous Adolpho gown and then run it over to The Very Dry Dry Cleaners so my Father could dry clean it and put it back on the rack in case anyone came in to pick it up, but it was gettin' kinda late so I decided to go straight to work. Well, I guess I was still daydreaming about The Inaugureagan 'cause when we pulled up at Rockefeller Center, it didn't register with me when the taxi-driver said,

> "No. No charge at all, Ms. Roseannadanna. You'll need the money more than me"

and drove off. So, I just continued humming "Hail to the Chief" as I walked into the lobby of the R_2CA Building and I was thinking what a beautiful day it was when all of a sudden I heard a burglar alarm go off and I saw this guy wearing a mask 'n holding a sack of money run right by me. It all happened so fast, it didn't register with me, but when this masked guy saw me, he stopped dead in his tracks and said,

> "Hey, Roseanne Roseannadanna, you're gonna be doin' this yourself pretty soon"

and then he ran away like a burglar. I thought to myself,

"What a crazy, crazy town . . ."

and I got on the elevator. The ride up was pretty uneventful except that the elevator operator and everyone else in the elevator was cryin' like babies. Naturally, I figured that it was because of the way I looked in my strapless, beaded, diaphanous Adolpho gown 'cause my whole staff was cryin' when they saw me too and they really started bawling their eyes out when I asked them who'd changed the locks to my office.

And then this weird feelin' started to come over me. I can't really explain what it was like, but I'll take a shot at it anyway. You see, I'm a street kid. I'm street smart. And call it a street cleaner's intuition if you want, but as I looked aroun' I couldn't help but notice the writing on the wall. I couldn't help but wake up 'n smell the coffee! I remember saying to myself,

"Hey, Roseanne, why is everythin' that used to be in your office now in boxes 'n crates in the hall outside your office? Like your desk 'n your lamp 'n your crushed-velvet armchair that you spilled the Orange Crush on that made some of the velvet all hard 'n crusty . . . 'n the NBC washcloth that you used to try 'n wash the crust off, 'n your NBC letter opener that you used to try 'n chisel that hard, crusty Crush off with, 'n your NBC tire patch that you ended up havin' to put over the hole you made with your NBC letter opener in your armchair . . . 'N where is your NBC washroom with with the NBC executive shower, 'n the NBC executive bidet, 'n the NBC executive toilet that still had a former NBC executive's crusty skidmarks at the bottom of it which made you so sick that you always used the public bathroom in the lobby."

*Estelle (Nanna) and Bert Roseannadanna, Sr.
with their first customer*

The Flying Bobarias

*From left to right: Bo Bobaria, Roseanne Maria Bobaria,
Carlotta Maria Bobaria, Uncle Bobo Bobaria, Aunt
Shirley, Bobo Bobaria, Jr.*

*My parents' wedding,
January 27, 1946*

*The Very Dry
Dry Cleaners*

Me, the tiny r.r.

**HERNANDO
ROSEANNADANDO**

**ROSEANNE
ROSEANNADANNA**

Ms. Lady Luck

The Rhyming Bum

Me and the editor of this book

David Brinkley

Me and Jane Curtin

Beverly Sills

Me and Walter Celery (NBC VP in charge of sign-offs) 1977

RCA Building

MY OFFICE WINDOW

NBC Peacock

Ronald Reagan

Me talking to Bo Derek

*President Reagan's
inaugural
buffet table*

Ron Reagan, Jr.

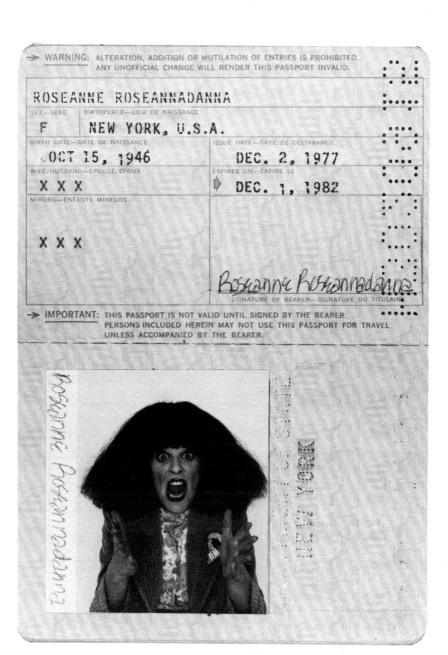

My passport

George Steinbrenner

Me, Roseanne Roseannadanna, typing this book

General George Patton

Yes. Somethin' started to register in my brain. Somethin' fishy was goin' on 'n I was gonna find out what it was. I went racing down the hall like a bull in a China Syndrome. You shoulda seen me! I was angrier than a maître d' who has to wear his work clothes to his daughter's formal wedding. I bursted open the doors to my boss' outer office, raced through the reception area, passed all the receptionists, bursted open the doors to the secretarial pool, raced past the secretaries, raced past their pool, bursted open the doors to his assistant's office, raced past his assistant, bursted through the doors to his waiting room, raced past eveyone who was waiting to see him, bursted through the doors to his office, raced past a couple o' peacocks, bursted through the doors to his private office, barged in and said,

"Hey, what's going on?"

My boss was a short middle-aged man (about 49 and about 4′9″) and he stood up and said,

"Sit down, Roseanne, I want to talk to you."

So I sat down. And he said,

"Are you comfortable, Roseanne? Can I get you a drink?"

I said,

"I don't drink! Everyone knows that!"

He said,

"So you don't. So you don't."

I said,

"No I don't. No I don't."

I smelled a rat. A small gray one with a long tail. It was lying in the corner of his office. I figured it was dead about three days.

> "Hey, it's 9:00 in the morning! Why are you offering me a drink at 9:00 in the morning?"

I asked as I stood up tryin' to show this guy that I meant business. My boss sat down 'n said,

> "I like you, Roseanne. You have a flair about you. You have a class and style that is all your own. And, most of all, you're a great journalist!"

> "Tell me somethin' I don't know!"

I said as I sat down. My boss stood up 'n said,

> "You're fired!"

> "What?"

I said as I stood up 'n said,

> "How come?"

He said,

> "Have a seat, Roseanne, I want to talk to you."

I said,

> "No. I can't take this sittin' down. Why am I fired?"

He said,

> "Well, you're not actually fired, Roseanne. We're just laying you off."

I said,

> "Why?"

He said,

> "REAGANOMETRY!"

I never heard of this before so I said,

> "You mean REAGANOMICS, don't you?"

He said,

> "No, REAGANOMETRY. It's like Reaganomics,
> but it's more complicated to explain. Do you
> have a protractor?"

I said,

> "No."

Who did he think I was, Sir Isaac Newton? Then he said,

> "Well, I just happen to have one here. Let me
> show you what I mean."

So with that, my short, middle-aged boss walked over to
the NBC blackboard, stood up on a chair, and started to
explain what REAGANOMETRY was,

> "Roseanne, if you have a 69-year-old President
> who stands at a 70° angle to the ground and
> who's understanding of the economy is that of a
> man who's I.Q. is 71, how many people will end
> up out of work?"

I answered,

> "11 million!"

My ex-boss shook his head 'n said,

> "11 million and one! Good-bye, Roseanne."

> "Hey. . ."

I said 'n he said,

> "I'm sorry, Roseanne, but with that many peo-
> ple unemployed, people are going to be too sad
> to watch the news. So we have to cut back. It's
> just a temporary thing. I hope. . . . And, who
> knows, maybe no news will be good news and
> maybe the good news will be that everybody's
> going back to work. But, there's really no telling
> when that'll happen . . . so . . . . the bad
> news is: Good-bye, Roseanne."

Well, I thought I was gonna die, but I figured I'd say a
couple o' dying words to this short guy,

> "You know, after all I've done for NBC, I just
> can't believe that this is the crummy way you'd
> break it to me."

He closed by sayin',

> "Well, we thought you'd take the hint from the
> sky-cap, or your taxi-driver, or the burglar, or
> this dead rat in my office, but I guess it just didn't
> register. Good-bye, Roseanne."

And just like that, it was over. Finished. Kaput. The
end. Finis. Sayonara. Au revoir. Shalom. Slam bam, no
thank you, Roseanne. Well, I was so depressed, I felt like
the former editor of this book. I didn't know what to do
with myself. I just left the RCA Building in a sort of daze 'n
started walking. Hey, talk about feelin' like you were left
at the altar! Here I was still wearin' the same strapless,

beaded, diaphanous Adolpho gown that I wore to the Inauguration of the same man that I got fired because of whose administration I just figured out would be known as The "Death Of A Salesman" Years.

I just kept walkin' 'n walkin' tryin' to figure out how all this happened and what I was gonna do about it. I mean how was I gonna tell my Father? He was so proud of me 'n my success 'n all the photos of world leaders he had hangin' on the walls of The Very Dry Dry Cleaners. He was always braggin' to everyone how all these hot-shots air-mailed their dirty clothes to him so that Roseanne Roseannadanna's Father could clean 'em. But, now I was really worried 'cause my Father had a history of high blood pressure and I was afraid he'd have a Roseannada-nuerism if he found out that his pride 'n joy not only didn't commute to work anymore, but didn't have any work to commute to. I couldn't tell him now. I couldn't even face him. Not just now, yet, anyway.

So, I just kept walkin' n' walkin' 'n as I did it started to register on me that people in the street were sayin' things like, "Sorry, Roseanne," 'n "Tough-break, Roseanne," 'n it made me feel worse 'n worse. You know, even though everyone knew who I was 'n I knew lots o' people, I felt alone. How was I gonna live? Let's face it, my life was my work 'n my work was my life. Then, I said out loud to myself,

> "If I don't have one, what's the sense of having the other?"

I guess I must've said that louder to myself than I thought 'cause right then 'n there, a mailman slapped me across the face 'n said,

> "Never say a thing like that! Not even as a joke! Here! I got a special delivery letter for you!"

And he handed me an envelope with my name on it. Then, he said,

> "You walk faster than anyone I ever knew. I
> started following you when you left Rockefeller
> Center and even though I was running, I can't
> believe that it took me until The Bronx to catch
> up with you!"

Well, needless to say I was as confused as Hitler must've
been when he heard that they were namin' the Adolpho
gown after him. But before I had a chance to ask him
what this was all about, the mailman shook his head 'n
said,

> "Don't ask me what this is all about 'cause I
> don't have time to explain 'cause I have to get
> back to my regular route. Too-Da-Loo!"

And just like that, like he was some winged-foot messen-
ger from Greek Mythology, the mailman, with his mailbag
floppin' against his side, started runnin' back towards
Manhattan.

So, there I was, the former Roseanne Roseannadanna,
out o' work 'n standin' on a cement sidewalk not too far
from Yankee Stadium in my strapless, beaded, diaphanous Adolpho gown holdin' this envelope with my ex-
name on it and bein' real pathetic. Then, all of a sudden,
some shopkeepers came outta their stores 'n started
yellin',

> "Hey Roseanne! Read the letter! Who's it from?
> Hey, quit being pathetic and read it! Maybe it's
> good news!"

So I figured what have I got to lose? So one of the
shopkeepers that owned a furniture store slid a chair
under me 'n I just sat right down there in the middle of the
sidewalk and opened the envelope. This is what was
inside:

January 21, 1981

Dear Roseanne Roseannadanna,

Hey! Look what's happened to me! I'm really cooking with gas! My family is good! My business is great! I moved outta New Jersey! I got a desk! I got new stationery! And I owe it all to you!

No! No! No! Don't try to be modest and say that I always had what it took to be a happy, successful guy who could have the world by the short 'n curlies if I just had a little confidence in myself. That might be true, but it was you, Roseanne Roseannadanna, who was always there when I needed you.

So, now that the tables are turned, I want to help you by giving you a great idea about what you should do with your life now that you're out o' work. And if you happen to be near a furniture store, tell the shopkeeper to start turning his tables 'cause here comes my GREAT IDEA!

Write a back to workbook! Isn't that a great idea? You could tell people who are out o' work how to get back to work!

Hey! I gotta run to a meeting about my new stationary. Let me know what you think of my GREAT IDEA!!

Sincerely,

Richard Feder

RF/rbz

Hey! It WAS a GREAT IDEA! And other people obviously thought so too 'cause the shopkeepers that were reading over my shoulder broke into an applause which was light 'n polite. Then, when other people who were passin' by asked them why they were standin' in the street clappin' their hands, the shopkeepers shouted,

"Roseanne's gonna write a book!"

and then all the passersby started clappin' 'n the clappin' got louder 'n louder until it turned into cheerin' 'n clappin' 'n before you knew it, there was such an ovation that George Steinbrenner came outta his office 'n said,

"I didn't know we had a game today."

But when someone told George that there wasn't a game 'n that all the ovating was because R_2 was gonna write a *"Hey, Get Back to Work!" Book* he started clappin' 'n cheerin' too.

Hey! I'm no fool. If this was the kind o' reaction that book was gettin' before I even decided to write it, I figured I should at least give it some thought. And I did give it lots o' thought. I thought about it for two years. You see at first I didn't feel like doin' it 'cause I was feelin' so lousy about everythin', but then I managed to get my spirits 'n my mental attitude 'n my physical condition back to a Roseannadanna peak. The kind o' peak that could give a gal the confidence to get back to work. And how in the world do you think I did that? Well, I accomplished this through certain tricks and devices that I will pass along to you, Mr./Mrs./Ms./Msq. Reader as soon as I write this, my *"Hey, Get Back to Work!" Book*. But, listen you guys. You don't have to take two years to get yourself together. You can learn from my experience and get started the minute you get fired with this great Roseannadanna-planna!

So, here goes! Ready or not, I'm gonna write this thing. And when I'm done with this book, I hope you read it. And after you read it, I hope you start clappin' 'n cheerin' too. I mean this is gonna be a hot 'n snappy get back to work book 'n by the time it comes out we'll all be (please God, knock wood, snatch your purse, purse your snatch) back to work!

Roseanne Roseannadanna
New York City, New York
1983

Roseanne Roseannadanna's "Hey, Get Back to Work!" Book

By Roseanne
Roseannadanna

With
Lots o' Help
from
Alan Zweibel
and
Gilda Radner

In Memory Of

General George Patton, my pet parakeet that died
when I was fourteen years old, but it really wasn't my
fault. Sure, I was the one that let him outta his cage
'cause he looked like he needed some exercise. And
sure, I was the one that was makin' whole wheat toast
in the kitchen 'cause I felt like I needed the roughage.
Okay. Okay. I also gotta admit that I was the one that
made the pitcher of Kool-Aid to help the roughage flush
outta my system anythin' that mighta been lyin' aroun'
in there. But I *wasn't* the one that rang the doorbell that
made me leave the kitchen to go answer the door. The
delivery boy did that. And I wasn't the one that told
General George Patton to fly on to the toaster, or to lick
one of those hot toaster coils, or to start chirpin' for
help, or to stiffen his little body, or to fall dead into my
pitcher of Kool-Aid. He did that all by himself.

Well, that little guy was my very first pet 'n I wanted to
give him a decent funeral. But it really wasn't my fault
that it didn't end up turnin' out that way. Sure, I was the
one that let the delivery boy pick up the pitcher that had
the Kool-Aid 'n the late General George Patton in it.
And sure, I was the one that showed the delivery boy
where our bathroom was. But I sure as hell wasn't the
one that started spillin' the Kool-Aid 'n General George
Patton into the toilet. The delivery boy did that. And,
(thank-God, thanks o' lot, pass the salt, pass the gas) I
wasn't the one that had to clean up after our toilet spilt

up General George Patton 'n what looked like two weeks o' stuff that I must've flushed outta my system 'n into the toilet's system. The plumbers in the hip boots did that. These guys also explained to me that it was pet fish that you bury in the toilet 'n pet birds you're s'posed to bury in your backyard. But I lived in the city 'n we didn't have a backyard. Anyways, me, the delivery boy, 'n the plumbers in the hip boots did the next best thing. We gave General George Patton a military funeral by dumpin' him into a red, white, 'n blue garbage can that was in front of an Army/Navy store. I hope the little General is gettin' lots o' rest in peace.

Table o' Contents

1.

You've Been Through A Lot

Hey, when you lost your job, you were prob'ly feelin' real depressed 'n dejected 'n rejected 'n subjected 'n objected to. I know *exactly* what you've been through. That's why we gotta get you back together again. We gotta inject lots o' confidence into *you!*

HERE'S HOW

1. Get up off the couch
2. Put your hands on your hips. (You look pretty snappy already.)
3. Now, take one hand off your hip and use it to pick up my book.
4. Walk over to the nearest mirror.
5. Say the following to yourself in the mirror:

"Hey, whatsa matter, Sparky? Life got you down? Have your best laid plans gone aft aglee? You down so low it looks like up to you? Cat got your tongue? Lou! Lou! Mr. Fields wants the rent! You draggin' your heels? You got egg on your face?

Yeah! I do got egg on my face! I had an egg for breakfast 'n there's a little, teeny, tiny piece of the yellow part on my face. What am I tryin' to do? Make myself sick?

NO!!!!

I'm tryin' to make myself happy 'n snappy again! 'Cause I'm okay! I'm hot stuff! I'm a good lookin', fast talkin', hot-shot guy/gal and I can have the world by the Moe, Larry, 'n Curlies if I just change my attitude. Yeah for me!

6. Wipe the mirror from where you fogged it up by talkin' so close.

2.
Get Some Sleep

You'll need it! 'Cause once you get back to work you'll be gettin' up at 6:00 AM 'n goin' to bed at 11:00 PM 'n gettin' up at 6:00 AM 'n goin' to bed at 11:00 PM 'n gettin' up at 6:00 AM again just like you did before you were out o' work. So, GET SOME SLEEP!

HERE'S HOW

1. Go to bed.
2. Now, get all cozy 'n sweet 'n tiny 'n snug as a bug in a rug 'n put powder under your arms 'n every-thin' 'n tuck yourself in all calm 'n tidy 'n warm 'n sweet 'n nice.
3. Close your eyes 'n go to sleep.
Don't worry. I'll wait. Where'm I gonna go? I don't have a job yet either . . . ZZZZZZZZZZZZZZZZZZ

ZZZZZZZZZZZ ZZZZZZZZZZZZZZZZZZZZ

ZZZ ZZZZZZZZZZZZZZ ZZZZZZZ

ZZZZZZZZZZZZZZZZ ZZZZZZZZZZZZZZ

ZZZZZZ ZZZZZZZZZZZZZZZZ ZZ

ZZZZZZZZZZZZZZZZZZZZZZ ZZZZZZZZZZ

ZZZZZZZZZZ ZZZZ ZZZZZSNOREZZZZZ

ZZSNOREZZZZZSNOREZZZZZSNOREZZZ Z ᴢ

3.

Good Morning

Did you have a nice sleep? I hope so. And now, have a good morning 'cause this is the first day of the rest o' your life 'n to everythin' there is a season turn, turn, turn 'n this is your season 'n this is your turn to turn.

HERE'S HOW

1. Just for no reason, start spinnin' aroun' 'n aroun' in your house. Then, start dancin' 'n turnin' 'n dippin' 'n jumpin' 'n twirlin' 'n spinnin'. Then, start laughin' 'n singin' 'n yellin' 'n whoopin' 'n roarin' 'n clappin'. Then, do everythin' all at once.

4.

Sit Down for a Minute

You're probably feelin' kind o' dizzy 'n nauseated from takin' your turn.

HERE'S HOW

1. Bend your knees.
2. Lower your . . . Come to think about it, if at this point in your life you have to be told how to sit, you don't deserve to vote, let alone have a job.

5.

Get Even More Confidence

Watch television for a couple o' days. There's always somethin' on television about someone in worse shape than you. Look closely in your *TV Guide* for these movies 'n shows that will invariably make you feel better about yourself:

1. *Brian's Song*
2. *The Elephant Man*
3. *Coma*
4. *First She Cries*
5. *Dark Victory*
6. *Yes, Georgio*
7. *Whose Life Is It, Anyway?*
8. *Love Story*
9. *I Never Promised You a Rose Garden*
10. *Old Yeller*
11. *Coming Home*
12. *"Quincy"*
13. *Anything about Roy Campanella*

6.
Connect These Dots

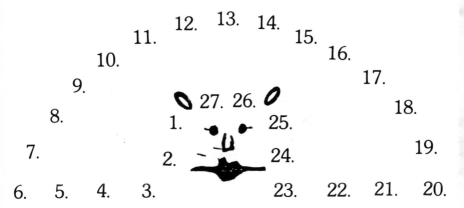

11. 12. 13. 14. 15.
10.   16.
9.   17.
8.   27. 26.   18.
   1.   25.
7.   2.   24.   19.
6. 5. 4. 3.   23. 22. 21. 20.

7.

Get Sick of Feelin' Sorry for Yourself

Let's face it, you can't sit aroun' the house forever. So, you gotta get sick of it! There are a lotta good ways of makin' yourself sick aroun' the house.

HERE'S HOW

1. Leave some of your nail-clippings on a desk.
2. Stick chewed gum 'n stuff from your nose under the dining room table 'n feel aroun' for it later.
3. Think about how those little pieces of red 'n brown 'n gray stuff are in the white sink while you are brushin' your teeth.
4. Leave an orange in a basket by the window for a couple o' weeks 'n watch it grow green fur.
5. Comb your hair with your bathmat.
6. Clean you ear with a Q-tip. Now, make yourself a very dry martini 'n stir it with the Q-tip.
7. Take about 4' of dental floss 'n attach one end of it to your kitchen wall 'n tape the other end of it to your refrigerator. When you are certain that it's secure, take anythin' that comes outta your landlord 'n hang it from the dental floss.
8. Take some stuff outta the corner of your dog's eye 'n put it in the corner of your eye.

9. Start rubbin' 'n scrapin' the inside of your ankle with your finger 'n fingernail until all that stuff that collects there rolls into a little ball. Now, do this to your other ankle, but this time make believe that it's Chubby Checker's foot.

10. Take all of the above stuff 'n put it in a blender. After you mix it aroun' for about a minute, pour the liquid into a brandy snifter. Now, take a deep breath. Now, count to ten. Now, splash it on your wall!

8.

Now, Get Up 'n Get Out 'n Get Another Job!!!!!!!

HERE'S HOW

1. Be snappy!
2. Be clean!
3. Be zippy!
4. Be dry!
5. Be hotsy!
6. Be totsy!
7. Bea Arthur!

Long Shadow Books

June 1, 1983

Ms. Roseanne Roseannadanna
c/o The Very Dry Dry Cleaners
Columbus Avenue
New York, New York 10024

Dear Ms. Roseannadanna:

I have just finished reading the Preface and the first eight chapters of your "HEY, GET BACK TO WORK!" BOOK, and I must say that I found it to be humorous, enlightening, and as delightfully unique as your "on camera" personna. The text has also been read by the various department heads here at Long Shadow Books, and I am pleased to report that they also share my enthusiasm.

Unfortunately, however, due to rising production costs which even we in publishing are feeling in these times of recession, our accountants tell me that it would be financially impractical for us to allow this project to extend beyond the one hundred pages that you were commissioned to write.

I am truly sorry, Ms. Roseannadanna. What I read was quite promising and gave every indication that the actual "how to" section of your "HEY, GET BACK TO WORK!" BOOK could have been quite intriguing had you had more pages to write them on. As disappointed as I am, I can't help but feel that had more thought been given to the body of the book than to the compelling, yet indulgent, preface, this situation would never have arisen.

In truth, this is all academic as we are scheduled to go to press on June 15th, and our accountants tell me that it would be financially impractical to delay publication in an attempt to correct this condition.

Sincerely,

Michael Greenstein

Michael Greenstein
Publisher

MG/tt

Simon & Schuster Building
1230 Avenue of the Americas
New York, NY 10020
212 246-2121
Published by Pocket Books
A Division of Simon & Schuster

25.

It's Always Something

Well, there you have it. I guess it just goes to show you, it's always something! If it's not one thing it's another. Either you're out o' work or the preface to your *"Hey, Get Back to Work!" Book* is twelve times longer than the rest o' your book.

But unless you're the kind o' person whose baby nurse accidently hit you in the head with a gumball machine, you must've figured out by now that all of this reminds me of a little song my ancestors used to sing all the time back in The Old Country. It's a patriotic tune that was written by my Uncle George M. Cohannadanna. It had such a snappy beat to it that in 1903, The Old Country adopted this song as it's National Roseannadanthem. All the people just loved to sing it. They sang it when they woke up. They sang it when they went to sleep. They sang it at a ballgame. They sang it before dinner 'n durin' dinner 'n after dinner. And, if they couldn't find the film-clip, they sang it on television right before it went off the air at night.

So since this book is just about ready to sign off the air, why don't you Mr./Mrs./Ms./Musical Reader stand at attention 'n sing this song which coincidentally is sung to the same tune as America's very own National Anthem:

HERE'S HOW

1. Sing this to the tune of "The Star-Spangled Banner."

Oh say can you see?
If you can't then you're blind
To the fact that we were
In the depths of recession.

Would you like some more soup?
Jobs are still hard to find.
I take back what I said,
'Twas a real depression.

But it didn't get worse
It went into reverse
At least, so they said . . .
Hey, who took my purse?

Oh say, should this star-spangled
Roseannabanner book not sell
Give your boss my resumé
Thanks o' lot, you've been swell.

Appendix

Did you ever think of how long it must take to do these appendix things? You gotta go back over the whole book 'n figure out what was where 'n put everthin' in alphabetical order 'n everythin'. I think it could make you into a nervous wreck. I mean I could hire someone to do it for me, but that would cut a chunk outta the money they're givin' me to write this thing. So, why don't we just skip the appendix part 'n if you can't find something or you want to look something up . . . either you could do it yourself or you can call me 'n I'll tell you where it is in the book. And don't call for just anythin'. Try 'n be considerate 'n make sure it's real important. Anyways, I hope you liked my book.

Good Night My Little/Mr./Mrs./

Ms. Reader,

Rosanne Rosannadanna

RESUME   ROSEANNE ROSEANNADANNA
                                c/o The Very Dry Dry Cleaners
                                Columbus Avenue
                                New York City, New York   10024
                                212-JL5-1001

NAME: ROSEANNE CHARLENE ROSEANNADANNA
AGE: 36
HAIR: Dark Brown
EYES: Brown
WEIGHT: Guess it 'n I'll give you a cigar.

EDUCATION:

ELEMENTARY SCHOOL: The Very Simple, Rudimentary, Elementary
                  My Dear Watson Elementary School

HIGH SCHOOL: Give The Little Lady A Drink And Put It On
                  My Bert Junior High School

COLLEGE: Columbia Broadcasting School

OUTSTANDING ACADEMIC ACHIEVEMENT:

Very Loud (99th Percentile)

LANGUAGES SPOKEN:

English
Broken English
Gibberish
Broken Gibberish

PREVIOUS WORK EXPERIENCE:

Go-Fer at NBC Network in New York City (1976)

Broadcast Journalist for NBC Television (1977-1981)

Toast O' The Town for New York City (1977-1981)

SPECIAL QUALIFICATIONS:

Confident
Snappy
Clean
Zippy
Happy
Witty
Hotsy
Totsy
Perky
Willing To Travel

REFERENCES: Anybody Who's Anybody.